THE ADVENTURES OF HUCKLEBERRY FINN

Mark Twain

AUTHORED by J. N. Smith
UPDATED AND REVISED by C. Shelby

COVER DESIGN by Table XI Partners LLC
COVER PHOTO by Olivia Verma and © 2005 GradeSaver, LLC

BOOK DESIGN by Table XI Partners LLC

Published by GradeSaver LLC, www.gradesaver.com

First published in the United States of America by GradeSaver LLC. 2000

GRADESAVER, the GradeSaver logo and the phrase "Getting you the grade since 1999" are registered trademarks of GradeSaver, LLC

ISBN 978-1-60259-002-1

Printed in the United States of America

For other products and additional information please visit http://www.gradesaver.com

Table of Contents

Table of Contents

Table of Contents

Biography of Mark Twain (1835–1910)

Christened as Samuel Langhorne Clemens, Mark Twain was born on November 30, 1835 in the small river town of Florida, Missouri, just 200 miles from Indian Territory. The sixth child of John Marshall Clemens and Jane Lampton, Twain lived in Florida, Missouri until the age of four, at which time his family relocated to Hannibal in hopes of improving their living situation.

By lineage, Twain was a Southerner, as both his parents' families hailed from Virginia. The slaveholding community of Hannibal, a river town with a population of 2000, provided a mix of rugged frontier life and the Southern tradition, a lifestyle that influenced Twain's later writings, including the *Adventures of Tom Sawyer*. Few black slaves actually resided in Hannibal, and the small farms on the delta were no comparison to the typical Southern plantation. In Hannibal, blacks were mostly held as household servants rather than field workers, but were still under the obligations of slavery.

In his youth, Twain was a mischievous boy, the prototype of his character, Tom Sawyer. Though he was plagued by poor health in his early years, by age nine he had already learned to smoke, led a small band of pranksters, and had developed an aversion to school. Twain's formal schooling ended after age 12, because his father passed away in March of that year. He became an apprentice in a printer's shop and then worked under his brother, Orion, at the Hannibal Journal, where he quickly became saturated in the newspaper trade. Rising to the role of sub–editor, Twain indulged in the frontier humor that flourished in journalism at the time: tall tales, satirical pranks, and jokes.

However, over the next few years, Twain found himself unable to save any wages and grew restless. He decided to leave Hannibal in June of 1853 and accepted a position in St. Louis. Soon afterwards, rather than settling in St. Louis, Twain proceeded to travel back and forth between New York, Philadelphia, Washington, and Iowa, working as a journalist. After his wanderings, Twain ultimately switched professions, realizing an old boyhood dream of becoming a river pilot.

Under the apprenticeship of Horace Bixby, pilot of the *Paul Jones*, Mark Twain became a licensed river pilot at the age of 24. Earning a high salary navigating the river waters, Twain was entertained by his work, and enjoyed his traveling lifestyle. In 1861, with the beginning of the Civil War, Twain's piloting days came to an end.

After returning home to Hannibal, Twain learned that military companies were being organized to assist Governor Jackson, and he enlisted as a Confederate soldier. Within a short period, he abandoned the cause, deserted the military, and along with thousands of other men avoiding the draft, moved West. On his way to Nevada, twelve years after the Gold Rush, Twain's primary intentions were to strike it rich mining for silver and gold. After realizing the impossibility of this dream, Twain once again picked up his pen and began to write.

Twain joined the staff of the Virginia City Territorial Enterprise, and became an established reporter/humorist. In 1863, he adopted the pseudonym Mark Twain, derived from a river pilot term describing safe navigating conditions. In 1869 he published his first book of travel letters entitled *Innocents Abroad*. The book was criticized widely and discouraged Twain from pursuing a literary career. In the years that followed, Twain published various articles, made lecture circuits, and relocated between San Francisco, New York, and Missouri. During this time he also met Olivia Langdon, whom he married on February 2, 1870. In November of the same year, their first son, Langdon Clemens, was born prematurely.

The Clemens family quickly fell into debt. However, when over 67,000 copies of *Innocents Abroad* sold within its first year, the American Publishing Company asked Twain for another book. Upon Olivia's request, the couple moved to the domicile town of Hartford, Connecticut, where Twain composed *Roughing It*, which documented the post–Gold Rush mining epoch and was published in 1872.

In March of 1872, Twain's daughter Susan Olivia was born, and the family appeared prosperous. Unfortunately, Langdon soon came down with Diphtheria and died. Twain was torn apart by his son's death, and blamed himself. Moreover, *Roughing It* was only mildly successful, which added to the family's hardships.

After traveling to Europe for a lecture series, Twain experienced a turning point in his career. Twain's newest novel, *The Gilded Age*, written in collaboration with Charles Dudley Warner, was published in 1873. The novel is about the 1800s era of corruption and exploitation at the expense of public welfare. *The Gilded Age* was Twain's first extended work of fiction and marked him in the literary world as an author rather than a journalist.

After the broad success of *The Gilded Age*, Twain began a period of concentrated writing. In 1880, his third daughter, Jean, was born. By the time Twain reached age fifty, he was already considered a successful writer and businessman. His popularity sky–rocketed with the publications of *The Adventures of Tom Sawyer* (1876), *The Prince and the Pauper* (1882), and *The Adventures of Huckleberry Finn* (1885). By 1885, Twain was considered one the greatest character writers in the literary community.

Twain died on April 21, 1910, having survived his children Langdon, Susan and Jean as well as his wife, Olivia. In his lifetime, he became a distinguished member of the literati, and was honored by Yale, the University of Missouri, and Oxford with literary degrees. With his death, many volumes of his letters, articles, and fables were published, including: *The Letters of Quintas Curtius Snodgrass* (1946); *Simon Wheeler, Detective* (1963); *The Works of Mark Twain: What is Man? and Other Philosophical Writings* (1973); and *Mark Twain's Notebooks and Journals* (1975–79). Perhaps more than any other classic American writer, Mark Twain is seen as a phenomenal author, but also as a personality that defined an era.

Other works include:

Punch, Brothers, Punch! and Other Stories (1878)

A Tramp Abroad (1880)

The Stolen White Elephant (1882)

Life on the Mississippi (1883)

A Connecticut Yankee in King Arthur's Court (1889)

Merry Tales (1892)

Personal Recollections of Joan of Arc (1896)

How to Tell a Story and Other Essays (1897)

A Dog's Tale (1904)

Is Shakespeare Dead? (1909)

Biography of Mark Twain (1835–1910)

About The Adventures of Huckleberry Finn

Throughout the twentieth century, *The Adventures of Huckleberry Finn* has become famous not only as one of Twain's greatest achievements, but also as a highly controversial piece of literature. In certain Southern states, the novel was banned due to its extensive criticism of the hypocrisy of slavery. Others have argued that the novel is racist due to the many appearances of the word "nigger." Unfortunately, the connotations of this word tend to override the novel's deeper antislavery themes, and prevent readers from understanding Twain's true perspective. In Twain's time, this word was used often and did not carry as powerful a racist connotation as it does currently. Therefore, in using the word, Twain was simply projecting a realistic portrayal of Southern society. Undoubtedly, *The Adventures of Huckleberry Finn* is highly significant due to its deep exploration of issues surrounding racism and morality, and continues to provide controversy and debate to this day, evidencing the continued relevance of these concepts.

Character List

Huck's name when the King pretends to be the British brother of Peter Wilks.

The lawyer who tries to ascertain the true heirs to the Wilks's fortune.

The false name the King uses when addressing Tim Collins, the young man bound for Orleans who tells the King everything about the Wilks family.

A drunk man who insults Colonel Sherburn and is later killed by him. The action takes place in the same town where the Duke and the King put on their Shakespearean show.

A young man who reveals the entire story about the Wilks's fortune to the King.

See The King

The widow who takes Huck into her home and tries to "civilize" him. It is her home that he leaves when Pap kidnaps him and takes him to the log cabin.

The younger of the two con men and the man who invents the Royal Nonesuch. He is later tarred and feathered in Pikesville.

The main character of the story. He runs away and travels down the Mississippi River on a raft with a runaway slave, Jim, as his companion.

A son of Col. Grangerford.

The youngest son of Col. Grangerford who becomes good friends with Huck but is later killed in the feud.

A daughter of Col. Grangerford.

The father of the Grangerford house and the man who invites Huck to live with the family. He is killed in the feud.

A daughter of the Grangerford's. She passed away before Huck's arrival, but used to create wonderful paintings and poetry.

The daughter of Col. Grangerford who runs off with Harney Shepherdson and rekindles the feud.

The eldest son of the Grangerford family.

The man who starts rallying a mob to kill Colonel Sherburn after Sherburn shoots and kills Boggs.

A member of Tom's robber band.

The false name Huck uses when he lives with the Grangerford's.

A runaway slave who accompanies Huck Finn down the Mississippi River.

The elder of the two con men with whom Huck is forced to travel. He plays the naked man in the Royal Nonesuch and is the man who sells Jim as a runaway slave. He is later tarred and feathered along with the Duke.

The woman whom Huck visits to gather news while pretending to be a girl. She tells him that she suspects Jim is hiding on Jackson's Island. Huck barely has time to get back to Jim and get them both off the island.

Tom Sawyer's uncle, and the farmer who purchases Jim from the King for forty dollars.

Tom's aunt who shows up at the end to find out what tricks Tom has been playing on her kinfolk. She reveals the true identities of Tom and Huck to her sister and spoils their attempt to steal Jim out of slavery by explaining he is already free.

The only man who recognizes that the King and Duke are frauds when they try to pretend to be British. He warns the town but they ignore him.

A member of Tom's robber band.

Tom Sawyer's younger brother. Tom pretends to be Sid while he and Huck Finn are living with Sally Phelps.

Huck Finn's best friend. Tom loves make believe games and sets up a band of robbers. Later he and Huck live together with Tom's Aunt Sally and Huck pretends to be Tom while Tom pretends to be his younger brother Sid.

The young man who runs away with Miss Sophia Grangerford.

Colonel Sherburn

An eminent citizen in the town who is respected and well—liked. He fights to protect Huck's money when Pap returns to claim Huck and steal his money.

One of the robbers on the shipwrecked steamboat.

The sister of the Widow Douglas. She tries to teach Huck how to read and write properly. Jim is her slave. He runs away from her after hearing that she wanted to sell him to a trader from down south.

The British brother of Peter Wilks whom the King impersonates until the real Harvey Wilks arrives.

The youngest daughter of the deceased George Wilks, she is distinguishable by her harelip.

The eldest daughter of the deceased George Wilks, a red—headed girl whom Huck starts to fall in love with. She becomes convinced that the King is her real uncle and not a fraud until Huck tells her the truth.

The dead man whose brother the King impersonates.

The second eldest daughter of the deceased George Wilks.

The British brother of Peter Wilks whom the Duke impersonates until the real William Wilks arrives.

Huck's abusive, alcoholic, broke father who returns early in the book to claim custody over him. When Huck can no longer take his father's abuse, he runs away and begins his journey down the river with Jim.

Major Themes

The primary theme of the novel is the conflict between civilization and "natural life." Huck represents natural life through his freedom of spirit, uncivilized ways, and desire to escape from civilization. He was raised without any rules or discipline and has a strong resistance to anything that might "sivilize" him. This conflict is introduced in the first chapter through the efforts of the Widow Douglas: she tries to force Huck to wear new clothes, give up smoking, and learn the Bible. Throughout the novel, Twain seems to suggest that the uncivilized way of life is more desirable and morally superior. Drawing on the ideas of Jean–Jacques Rousseau, Twain suggests that civilization corrupts, rather than improves, human beings.

The theme of honor permeates the novel after first being introduced in the second chapter, where Tom Sawyer expresses his belief that there is a great deal of honor associated with thieving. Robbery appears throughout the novel, specifically when Huck and Jim encounter robbers on the shipwrecked boat and are forced to put up with the King and Dauphin, both of whom "rob" everyone they meet. Tom's original robber band is paralleled later in the novel when Tom and Huck become true thieves, but honorable ones, at the end of the novel. They resolve to steal Jim, freeing him from the bonds of slavery, which is an honorable act. Thus, the concept of honor and acting to earn it becomes a central theme in Huck's adventures.

Food plays a prominent role in the novel. In Huck's childhood, he often fights pigs for food, and eats out of "a barrel of odds and ends." Thus, providing Huck with food becomes a symbol of people caring for and protecting him. For example, in the first chapter, the Widow Douglas feeds Huck, and later on Jim becomes his symbolic caretaker, feeding and watching over him on Jackson's Island. Food is again discussed fairly prominently when Huck lives with the Grangerford's and the Wilks's.

A theme Twain focuses on quite heavily on in this novel is the mockery of religion. Throughout his life, Twain was known for his attacks on organized religion. Huck Finn's sarcastic character perfectly situates him to deride religion, representing Twain's personal views. In the first chapter, Huck indicates that hell sounds far more fun than heaven. Later on, in a very prominent scene, the "King", a liar and cheat, convinces a religious community to give him money so he can "convert" his pirate friends. The religious people are easily led astray, which mocks their beliefs and devotion to God.

Superstition appears throughout the novel. Generally, both Huck and Jim are very rational characters, yet when they encounter anything slightly superstitious, irrationality takes over. The power superstition holds over the two demonstrates that Huck and Jim are child–like despite their apparent maturity. In addition, superstition foreshadows the plot at several key junctions. For instance, when Huck spills salt, Pap returns, and when Huck touches a snakeskin with his bare hands, a rattlesnake bites Jim.

The theme of slavery is perhaps the most well known aspect of this novel. Since it's first publication, Twain's perspective on slavery and ideas surrounding racism have been hotly debated. In his personal and public life, Twain was vehemently anti–slavery. Considering this information, it is easy to see that *The Adventures of Huckleberry Finn* provides an allegory to explain how and why slavery is wrong. Twain uses Jim, a main character and a slave, to demonstrate the humanity of slaves. Jim expresses the complicated human emotions and struggles with the path of his life. To prevent being sold and forced to separate from his family, Jim runs away from his owner, Miss Watson, and works towards obtaining freedom so he can buy his family's freedom. All along their journey downriver, Jim cares for and protects of Huck, not as a servant, but as a friend. Thus, Twain's encourages the reader to feel sympathy and empathy for Jim and outrage at the society that has enslaved him and threatened his life. However, although Twain attacks slavery through is portrayal of Jim, he never directly addresses the issue. Huck and Jim never debate slavery, and all the other slaves in the novel are very minor characters. Only in the final section of the novel does Twain develop the central conflict concerning slavery: should Huck free Jim and then be condemned to hell? This decision is life–altering for Huck, as it forces him to reject everything "civilization" has taught him. Huck chooses to free Jim, based on his personal experiences rather than social norms, thus choosing the morality of the "natural life" over that of civilization.

The concept of wealth or lack thereof is threaded throughout the novel, and highlights the disparity between the rich and poor. Twain purposely begins the novel by pointing out that Huck has over six thousand dollars to his name; a sum of money that dwarfs all the other sums mentioned, making them seem inconsequential in contrast. Huck demonstrates a relaxed attitude towards wealth, and because he has so much of it, does not view money as a necessity, but rather as a luxury. Huck's views regarding wealth clearly contrast with Jim's. For Jim, who is on a quest to buy his family out of slavery, money is equivalent to freedom. In addition, wealth would allow him to raise his status in society. Thus, Jim is on a constant quest for wealth, whereas Huck remains apathetic.

The majority of the plot takes place on the river or its banks. For Huck and Jim, the river represents freedom. On the raft, they are completely independent and determine their own courses of action. Jim looks forward to reaching the free states, and Huck is eager to escape his abusive, drunkard of a father and the "civilization" of Miss Watson. However, the towns along the river bank begin to exert influence upon them, and eventually Huck and Jim meet criminals, shipwrecks, dishonesty, and great danger. Finally, a fog forces them to miss the town of Cairo, at which point there were planning to head up the Ohio River, towards the free states, in a steamboat.

Originally, the river is a safe place for the two travelers, but it becomes increasingly dangerous as the realities of their runaway lives set in on Huck and Jim. Once reflective of absolute freedom, the river soon becomes only a short-term escape, and the novel concludes on the safety of dry land, where, ironically, Huck and Jim find their true freedom.

Short Summary

The Adventures of Huckleberry Finn is often considered Twain's greatest masterpiece. Combining his raw humor and startlingly mature material, Twain developed a novel that directly attacked many of the traditions the South held dear at the time of its publication. Huckleberry Finn is the main character, and through his eyes, the reader sees and judges the South, its faults, and its redeeming qualities. Huck's companion Jim, a runaway slave, provides friendship and protection while the two journey along the Mississippi on their raft.

The novel opens with Huck telling his story. Briefly, he describes what he has experienced since, *The Adventures of Tom Sawyer*, which preceded this novel. After Huck and Tom discovered twelve thousand dollars in treasure, Judge Thatcher invested the money for them. Huck was adopted by the Widow Douglas and Miss Watson, both of whom took pains to raise him properly. Dissatisfied with his new life, and wishing for the simplicity he used to know, Huck runs away. Tom Sawyer searches him out and convinces him to return home by promising to start a band of robbers. All the local young boys join Tom's band, using a hidden cave for their hideout and meeting place. However, many soon grow bored with their make–believe battles, and the band falls apart.

Soon thereafter, Huck discovers footprints in the snow and recognizes them as his violent, abusive Pap's. Huck realizes Pap, who Huck hasn't seen in a very long time, has returned to claim the money Huck found, and he quickly runs to Judge Thatcher to "sell" his share of the money for a "consideration" of a dollar. Pap catches Huck after leaving Judge Thatcher, forces him to hand over the dollar, and threatens to beat Huck if he ever goes to school again.

Upon Pap's return, Judge Thatcher and the Widow try to gain court custody of Huck, but a new judge in town refuses to separate Huck from his father. Pap steals Huck away from the Widow's house and takes him to a log cabin. At first Huck enjoys the cabin life, but after receiving frequent beatings, he decides to escape. When Pap goes into town, Huck seizes the opportunity. He saws his way out of the log cabin, kills a pig, spreads the blood as if it were his own, takes a canoe, and floats downstream to Jackson's Island. Once there, he sets up camp and hides out.

A few days after arriving on the island, Huck stumbles upon a still smoldering campfire. Although slightly frightened, Huck decides to seek out his fellow inhabitant. The next day, he discovers Miss Watson's slave, Jim, is living on the island. After overhearing the Widow's plan to sell him to a slave trader, Jim ran away. Jim, along with the rest of the townspeople, thought Huck was dead and is frightened upon seeing him. Soon, the two share their escape stories and are happy to have a companion.

While Huck and Jim live on the island, the river rises significantly. At one point, an entire house floats past them as they stand near the shore. Huck and Jim climb aboard to see what they can salvage and find a dead man lying in the corner of the house. Jim goes over to inspect the body and realizes it is Pap, Huck's father. Jim keeps this information a secret.

Soon afterwards, Huck returns to the town disguised as a girl in order to gather some news. While talking with a woman, he learns that both Jim and Pap are suspects in his murder. The woman then tells Huck that she believes Jim is hiding out on Jackson's Island. Upon hearing her suspicions, Huck immediately returns to Jim and together they flee the island to avoid discovery.

Using a large raft, they float downstream during the nights and hide along the shore during the days. In the middle of a strong thunderstorm, they see a steamboat that has crashed, and Huck convinces Jim to land on the boat. Together, they climb aboard and discover there are three thieves on the wreck, two of whom are debating whether to kill the third. Huck overhears this conversation, and he and Jim try to escape, only to find that their raft has come undone from its makeshift mooring. They manage to find the robbers' skiff and immediately take off. Within a short time, they see the wrecked steamship floating downstream, far enough below the water–line to have drowned everyone on board. Subsequently, they reclaim their original raft, and continue down the river with both the raft and the canoe.

As Jim and Huck continue floating downstream, they become close friends. Their goal is to reach Cairo, where they can take a steamship up the Ohio River and into the free states. However, during a dense fog, with Huck in the canoe and Jim in the raft, they are separated. When they find each other in the morning, it soon becomes clear that in the midst of the fog, they passed Cairo.

A few nights later, a steamboat runs over the raft, and forces Huck and Jim to jump overboard. Again, they are separated as they swim for their lives. Huck finds the shore and is immediately surrounded by dogs. After managing to escape, he is invited to live with a family called the Grangerford's. At the Grangerford home, Huck is treated well and discovers that Jim is hiding in a nearby swamp. Everything is peaceful until an old family feud between the Grangerford's and the Shepherdson's is rekindled. Within one day all the men in the Grangerford family are killed, including Huck's new best friend, Buck. Amid the chaos, Huck runs back to Jim, and together they start downriver again.

Further downstream, Huck rescues two humbugs known as the Duke and the King. Immediately, the two men take control of the raft and start to travel downstream, making money by cheating people in the various towns along the river. The Duke and the King develop a scam they call the Royal Nonesuch, which earns them over four hundred dollars. The scam involves getting all the men in the town to come to a show with promises of great entertainment. In the show, the King parades around naked for a few minutes. The men are too ashamed to admit to wasting their money, and tell everyone else that the show was phenomenal, thus making the following night's performance a success. On the third night, everyone returns plotting revenge, but the Duke and King manage to escape with all their ill gotten gains.

Further downriver, the two con men learn about a large inheritance meant for three recently orphaned girls. To steal the money, the men pretend to be the girls' British uncles. The girls are so happy to see their "uncles" that they do not realize they are being swindled. Meanwhile, the girls treat Huck so nicely that he vows to protect them from the con men's scheme. Huck sneaks into the King's room and steals the large bag of gold from the inheritance. He hides the gold in Peter Wilks's (the girls' father) coffin. Meanwhile, the humbugs spend their time liquidating the Wilks family property. At one point, Huck finds Mary Jane Wilks, the eldest of the girls, and sees that she is crying. He confesses the entire story to her. She is infuriated, but agrees to leave the house for a few days so Huck can escape.

Right after Mary Jane leaves, the real Wilks uncles arrive in town. However, because they lost their baggage on their voyage, they are unable to prove their identities. Thus, the town lawyer gathers all four men to determine who is lying. The King and the Duke fake their roles so well that there is no way to determine the truth. Finally, one of the real uncles says his brother Peter had a tattoo on his chest and challenges the King to identify it. In order to determine the truth, the townspeople decide to exhume the body. Upon digging up the grave, the townspeople discover the missing money Huck hid in the coffin. In the ensuing chaos, Huck runs straight back to the raft and he and Jim push off into the river. The Duke and King also escape and catch up to rejoin the raft.

Farther down the river, the King and Duke sell Jim into slavery, claiming he is a runaway slave from New Orleans. Huck decides to rescue Jim, and daringly walks up to the house where Jim is being kept. Luckily, the house is owned by none other than Tom Sawyer's Aunt Sally. Huck immediately pretends to be Tom. When the real Tom arrives, he pretends to be his younger brother, Sid Sawyer. Together, he and Huck contrive a plan to help Jim escape from his "prison," an outdoor shed. Tom, always the troublemaker, also makes Jim's life difficult by putting snakes and spiders into his room.

After a great deal of planning, the boys convince the town that a group of thieves is planning to steal Jim. That night, they collect Jim and start to run away. The local farmers follow them, shooting as they run after them. Huck, Jim, and Tom manage to escape, but Tom is shot in the leg. Huck returns to town to fetch a doctor, whom he sends to Tom and Jim's hiding place. The doctor returns with Tom on a stretcher and Jim in chains. Jim is treated badly until the doctor describes how Jim helped him take care of the boy. When Tom awakens, he demands that they let Jim go free.

At this point, Aunt Polly appears, having traveled all the way down the river. She realized something was very wrong after her sister wrote to her that both Tom and Sid had arrived. Aunt Polly tells them that Jim is indeed a free man, because the Widow had passed away and freed him in her will. Huck and Tom give Jim forty dollars for being such a good prisoner and letting them free him, while in fact he had been free for quite some time.

After this revelation, Jim tells Huck to stop worrying about his Pap and reveals that the dead man in the floating house was in fact Huck's father. Aunt Sally offers to adopt Huck, but he refuses on the grounds that he had tried that sort of lifestyle once before, and it didn't suit him. Huck concludes the novel stating he would never have undertaken the task of writing out his story in a book, had he known it would take so long to complete.

Summary and Analysis of Chapter 1 to Chapter 5

Summary

Chapter 1

The Adventures of Huckleberry Finn begins where the The Adventures of Tom Sawyer leaves off. At the end of the previous novel, Huck and Tom find a treasure of twelve thousand dollars, which they divide. Judge Thatcher takes their money and invests it in the bank at six percent interest, so that each boy earns a dollar a day on their money. Huck Finn moves in with the Widow Douglas, who has agreed to care for him.

Huckleberry Finn is the narrator of this story, and he starts off by describing his life to the reader. After moving in with the Widow Douglas, who buys him new clothes and begins teaching him the Bible. Huck is uncomfortable with all of these "restrictions" on his life, and soon runs away to avoid being "civilized". Tom Sawyer goes after Huck and convinces him to return to the Widow's house after promising that they will start a band of robbers together. Huck agrees to return, but still complains about having to wear new clothes and eat only when the dinner bell rings, something he was not used to while growing up with his Pap.

The Widow Douglas teaches Huck the Bible and forbids him from smoking. Her attentions towards him are complemented by her sister, Miss Watson, who also lives in the house. Miss Watson is a spinster who decides that Huck must get an education. She tries to teach him spelling and lectures him on how to behave well so that he will be welcomed into heaven. Miss Watson warns Huck that if he does not change his ways, he will go to hell. Ironically, Huck finds the description of hell far more enticing and exciting than the description of heaven, and decides he would rather go to hell, but doesn't tell Miss Watson of his decision.

That night, Huck goes into his bedroom and lights a candle before falling asleep. He starts to feel very lonely and equates every night sound, including an owl, dog and whippowill, with death. At one point, Huck flicks a spider away, and accidentally burns it up in the candle flame, which he thinks is a very bad omen. Huck lies awake until midnight, at which time he hears a soft meow from below his window. The meow is a signal from Tom Sawyer, and Huck replies with a similar meow. He climbs out of the bedroom window and drops to the ground to meet his friend.

Chapter 2

While the boys are sneaking away, Huck trips over a root and makes a noise when he falls. Miss Watson's slave Jim hears the sound and comes outside to look around. Huck and Tom hunker down to hide, and Jim ends up sitting down right between them to wait to hear the sound again. At first, Huck thinks they will never get away, but Jim soon gets tired and falls asleep against a tree.

While Jim sleeps, Tom wants to play a trick on him. He and Huck climb into the house and steal three candles, for which they leave a nickel as "pay". Then Tom quietly makes his way to Jim, takes off Jim's hat, and places it on a tree branch above Jim's head. He soon returns and tells Huck what he did.

After Jim wakes up, he believes he has been bewitched, and keeps the nickel as a token around his neck for the rest of his life. According to Huck, Jim tells all the other slaves that he had been ridden around the world by some witches, and that the nickel was given to him by the devil.

Tom and Huck sneak down to the river and meet some of the other boys who are supposed to be members of Tom's robber band. Together, they steal a skiff and float down the river several miles to an area where Tom has discovered a cave. Tom shows the boys a hidden room in the cave which they make their robber headquarters. Tom then reads them an oath that he has written, taken mostly from robber books and pirate stories. The boys argue over what Huck Finn's role in the gang will be, because Huck does not have a family for them to kill in case he reveals any of the gang's secrets. Huck finally offers them Miss Watson in place of his real parents, and the boys then sign an oath in blood to join the band. Tom is elected captain.

Tom explains that as robbers, they will only attack carriages and take the things inside. The men will be killed and the women will be brought back to the cave. He also mentions that they will ransom some of the people, because that is what they do in books, although he has no idea what "ransom" means. After that, all the boys agree to meet again soon. They return home exhausted and Huck climbs into bed having muddied up his new clothes, and feeling dead tired.

Chapter 3

The morning after his robber gang adventure, Huck receives a lecture from Miss Watson for dirtying his clothes. She takes him into a closet to pray, and tells him to pray every day so he will get what he wants. Huck tries to pray daily, but becomes disillusioned when all he gets is a fish–line with no hooks, when he prayed extra hard for hooks. When he asks Miss Watson about it, she tells him praying brings spiritual gifts. Unable to see any use for that sort of thing, Huck decides praying is probably not worth his time.

A drowned man is found in the river, and the townspeople believe is Huck's Pap. Huck is unconvinced after he hears the man was found floating on his back. He remarks that everyone knows dead men float face down, so this must have been a woman in man's clothing that looked like his Pap.

Tom Sawyer's robber band falls apart after a few weeks because the boys get bored of pretending they are robbing people. The only real escapade is when they wreck a Sunday School picnic and chase some of elementary school children away. Tom pretends that during this 'battle' there were Arabs and elephants and that the boys were attacking a large army, but Huck is too practical to follow Tom's fantastical imaginations. When Huck asks why they could not see all the elephants, Tom explains that some magicians must have turned the whole army into a Sunday School picnic. Tom then tells Huck all about genies in bottles, and how the genies must obey whoever rubs the bottle. Huck gets an old lamp and tries to find a genie, but when it fails he decides that the genies were just another of Tom's lies.

Chapter 4

Huck spends the next three months living with the widow and getting acclimated to his new life. He starts to attend school and remarks, "I liked the old ways best, but I was getting so I liked the new ones, too."

Everything goes fairly well until one day when Huck accidentally overturns a salt–shaker at the breakfast table. Miss Watson does not let him throw any salt over his left shoulder (as a way of avoiding the bad luck), and as a result Huck starts to get worried that something bad will happen. As soon as Huck leaves the house, he notices boot prints in the fresh snow. Upon closer inspection he realizes that there is a cross on the left boot–heel, which he has only ever seen in his Pap's. Huck's Pap has returned.

Aware that Pap is probably after his money (the $6,000 that he got from sharing the treasure with Tom), Huck goes to Judge Thatcher and begs the Judge to take all his money as a gift. The Judge is quite surprised by the request, but when Huck refuses to reveal why he wants to give away his money, Judge Thatcher agrees to "buy" it for one dollar, saying he will take the money "for a consideration."

Huck, still quite worried over what is going to happen now that Pap has returned, goes to the Miss Watson's slave Jim for advice. Jim takes out a hair–ball in order to do some magic with it for Huck. When the hair–ball refuses to work properly, Jim suggest that Huck give it some money. Huck offers a counterfeit quarter, which Jim takes and places under the ball. Jim tells Huck that Pap is torn between two angels, a good white angel and a bad black angel. He also explains that Huck will have considerable pain in his life and at the same time considerable joy. Huck returns to his room that night and finds his Pap sitting there.

Chapter 5

Huck arrives back at his room and sees his Pap sitting in a chair. Huck describes Pap as a filthy, poor man who used to scare him a great deal. Now, however, Huck is no longer scared of Pap, and instead notes how old his father has grown.

Pap harasses Huck for wearing good clothes and going to school. He then accuses Huck of putting on airs and acting better than his own father. Pap remarks that no one in his family could ever read, and that he certainly does not want his son to be smarter than he is. He demands that Huck read him something, and soon becomes quite furious when he realizes that Huck is in fact able to read. Pap threatens to beat Huck if he ever catches him near the school again. He makes Huck hand over the dollar that Judge Thatcher "paid" him and then climbs out the window to go drinking in the town.

The next day, Pap goes to Judge Thatcher and tries to make the Judge give him Huck's money. The Judge refuses, and he and the widow take a case to court in an effort to get Huck legally placed with one of them. The custody judge is unfortunately new to the town and refuses to separate Huck from his father. Judge Thatcher, realizing he cannot win, gives Huck some money, which Huck immediately turns over to Pap. Pap gets extremely drunk and is placed in jail for a week.

The new judge then sympathetically takes Pap into his home, dresses him well, and tries to reform him. After thinking that he has reformed Pap, the Judge goes to bed. That night, Pap sneaks out of the new judge's house and buys some alcohol. By morning he is so drunk that he breaks his arm in two places and nearly freezes to death on the porch. The new judge is livid at this betrayal of his trust and comments that the only way to reform Pap is with a shotgun.

Analysis

The first sentence introduces Huck in a colloquial, friendly manner: "You don't know about me." From the very first words of the novel, Twain makes it clear that Huck is the narrator, and that the reader will hear the story of his adventures directly from him. In addition, to make it clear to readers unfamiliar with *The Adventures of Tom Sawyer* that this novel exists independently, Huck explains that if they haven't read Twain's earlier work, it "ain't no matter."

The Widow Douglas is an honorable woman who hopes to nurture Huck into a civilized child. Here, the reader immediately understands the main theme of the novel, the conflict between civilization and freedom. In agreement with Rousseau, Twain tends to suggest that civilization corrupts rather than improves human beings. For example, in the first chapter, Huck is forced to change his natural character into the mold the Widow Douglas demands from him. He feels cramped in new clothes, and hates being limited to eating dinner only when the dinner bell rings. Twain cleverly contrasts this new lifestyle with Huck's old way of life. For example, Huck compares eating dinner off a plate to eating from a "barrel of odds and ends," which implies a pig's slop bucket. Here, Twain explains that in his earlier life, Huck competed for food with pigs, but also notes that Huck enjoyed eating from the slop bucket more than eating from the plate. Huck's relationship with food is a prominent theme throughout the novel, and during his time on Jackson's Island and working his way down river, Huck revels in and enjoys his ad hoc dining.

In the first chapter, we observe Huck is ironically trapped in a "civilized" world, when he would prefer to live freely in nature. Irony appears in other areas of the novel as well. For example, Huck explains that the Widow Douglas wouldn't let him smoke, even though, ironically, she secretly uses snuff herself. Irony appears yet again when Miss Watson tries to warn Huck about hell. This warning is juxtaposed by her painful academic lessons. Huck finds spelling very difficult to learn and hates the lessons so much, that he remarks hell sounds more enjoyable. In this ironic reference, Twain reminds the reader of Huck's childhood innocence. Only a child would rationally choose hell over heaven.

Superstition permeates the novel. The first chapter provides several examples of Huck's superstitious side, specifically in his interpretation of the night sounds (as death), and in how he believes the spider burning to death in the flame of his candle is a serious omen of bad luck. After killing the spider, Huck immediately attempts a counter–charm, even though he knows there is no way of undoing bad luck.

Typically, Huck is a very sensible person, making his adherence to superstition slightly ironic. Huck is very logical and reasonable. For example, in determining that he would prefer heaven over hell after Miss Watson describes the two to him, Huck uses very logical reasoning that the reader can understand. Superstition, on the other hand, is completely irrational. Thus, when confronted by superstition Huck behaves contrary to his usual manner, perhaps a reminder that he is just a child, or an allusion to typical sensibilities of the time. Moreover, superstition symbolizes Huck's fear of the unknown; Huck is most superstitious whenever he is extremely worried about his future, such as in this opening chapter and later while on Jackson's Island. Superstition also serves to foreshadow events throughout the novel, as Huck knows the bad luck will return to haunt him. For example, after Huck accidentally brushes the spider into his candle flame, Pap returns to town.

This chapter serves to introduce the other boys in Huck's town. It is important to notice that although Huck Finn and Tom Sawyer are best friends, the other boys are more than willing to cut Huck out of Tom's gang. Understanding that Huck is not very popular helps explain his feelings of isolation in the town; the adults keep trying to "sivilize" him, and the other boys tend to ignore him.

Here, Twain interestingly juxtaposes theft and honor. These contradictory ideas are conveniently merged by Tom Sawyer, who logically explains to the other boys that robbery is honorable. Tom's definition appears to be complete nonsense. However, as the reader will see by the end of the book, this scene actually parallels the novel's ending, where Huck and Tom "steal" Jim out of slavery. Thus, Twain truly demonstrates how honor and robbery can coexist.

Tom Sawyer's gang can be viewed as a childish representation of society as a whole, an example of a synecdoche. Tom creates a set of rules, ideas, and morals that he expects the boys to adhere to, all of which he gets from books. Thus, books form a foundation for civilization; using books, Tom creates a society for his gang of friends. Ironically, Twain mocks the adult world in this chapter by showing that although the adult world relies on books such as the Bible to define civilization, pirate and robber books might also suffice.

Slavery is introduced in this chapter through Tom and Huck's interactions with Miss Watson's slave, Jim. As the novel progresses, slavery gradually becomes a larger issue. It is important to note Huck's views towards slavery at this point so that they may be compared to his views later on. In this chapter, Huck comments that Jim, "was most ruined, for a servant," thus demonstrating he supports the idea of slavery. Only later in the novel does Huck start to question whether Jim should be a servant at all.

Huck's rationality and literalness appear here. Twain goes to great lengths to show that Huck is a logical thinker who only believes what he can see with his own eyes. Thus, Tom's band becomes boring when all they do is attack turnip wagons and Sunday School picnics. Unlike Tom Sawyer, Huck is unable to make–believe that the picnic is really an Arab army. The same thing happens with respect to Huck's Pap; Huck decides that Pap cannot be dead because the dead person was floating on its back rather than its face, meaning that it must have been a woman.

This focus on rationality and literalness is used by Twain to further attack religion. Huck is told to pray for what he wants, but when he prays and does not get anything, he decides that praying is pointless. Huck also thinks about the Christian concept of always helping other people. When he realizes that Christianity seems to offer him no personal advantage in life, he quickly rejects it as quite pointless.

Superstition appears again when Huck asks Jim to help him decide what to do about Pap. Jim uses a large hairball he believes to have magical abilities to help Huck. This is the first time that Twain foreshadows the happenings of the rest of the novel. Jim mentions "two gals flyin'" around Huck's life, a light one and a dark one, a rich one and a poor one. This is of course a reference to Huck and to Jim, since Huck is rich and Jim is poor. Jim's comment that Huck should avoid the water will go unheeded when both of them end up running away downriver.

Huck reinforces a split between what can be termed "natural learning" versus "book learning." He has been brought up with only "natural learning," such as how to survive in the wild. This can be contrasted with Tom Sawyer's "book learning," which has little actual application in Huck's life, and which Twain makes fun of by portraying the silliness of Tom's robber band. The usefulness of Huck's type of learning is constantly tested, for instance when he spots Pap's boot marks in the snow. This split between natural and book learning will be brought to a head when Huck encounters Pap directly.

Summary and Analysis of Chapter 6 to Chapter 10

Summary

Chapter 6

Pap begins hanging out around the town and demands Huck give him money every few days. When the widow tells Pap to get away from her property, he kidnaps Huck and takes him three miles upriver to a log cabin. Pap carefully locks the door and never leaves Huck's side without making sure that Huck cannot escape. Huck enjoys being free from school but soon gets upset that he is being beaten so much.

Searching for a way to escape, Huck discovers part of a saw that is missing its handle and starts to saw off a log in the rear corner of the cabin, but is forced to stop when Pap returns. Pap is drunk and makes Huck go outside and bring in all the supplies he has brought from town. Pap proceeds to drunkenly curse everyone he has ever met and spends a significant part of his tirade criticizing the government.

Huck hopes to escape after Pap falls asleep, but Pap has a fitful night, and Huck is afraid he might wake up and catch him trying to get out of the cabin. At one point Pap jumps up thinking he is covered with snakes. Later, he dreams that the angel of death is after him and he starts to chase Huck around the cabin with a knife. Huck runs for his life and manages to survive after Pap falls asleep again. Huck then takes down the gun and holds it for protection.

Chapter 7

Pap and Huck go out into the woods to hunt for game. While there, Huck sees an abandoned canoe on the river and jumps in to get it. When he realizes that Pap did not see him snare the canoe, he hides it in a little stream for future use and returns to Pap. Next, Huck fetches a wooden raft from the river with timber that is worth about ten dollars. Pap locks Huck into the cabin and takes the raft to town in order to sell it.

Taking advantage of Pap's absence, Huck quickly finishes his sawing and climbs out of the cabin, taking everything worth any money to his canoe. He axes down the front door and goes hunting for game. Huck shoots a wild pig, butchers it inside the cabin, and spreads the blood on his shirt and the floor. He also carefully lays some of his hairs on the now bloody ax to make it appear as if he has been killed. Huck cuts open a sack of flour and marks a trail indicating that the killer left via a lake that does not connect to the river. Thus, he prevents anyone from searching along the river for anything more than his dead body.

As Huck is finishing, a man appears nearby in a skiff. Huck recognizes that it is Pap returning early and that he is sober. Immediately, Huck jumps into the canoe and pushes off. He floats downstream until he reaches Jackson's Island, a deserted stretch of land in the middle of the river. Huck ties up the canoe and satisfied with his work, settles down to get some sleep.

Chapter 8

Huck wakes up on Jackson's Island late the next day and hears a cannon being fired. A ferryboat filled with his friends comes down the river firing a cannon in hopes of bringing his dead body to the surface. The search parties have also set loaves of bread filled with mercury afloat, believing the mercury and bread will be attracted to his body. Knowing the loaves will be floating around the area, Huck searches for one and enjoys eating it for lunch.

After a few days, Huck begins exploring the island. While following and hunting a large snake, he accidentally stumbles into a clearing with a still smoking campfire. Out of fear, he retreats to his campsite and paddles over to the Illinois side of the river. However, he soon returns for the night and sleeps poorly as he is overwhelmed with fear for who else might be inhabiting the island.

The next morning Huck decides to find out who else is on the island with him. He paddles his canoe down to the other campsite and hides in the brush. Soon he sees Jim, the slave Tom Sawyer played tricks on. Out of joy for finding a friend on the island, Huck rushes out and greets him. Jim nearly dies of fright when he sees Huck, whom he believes to be dead. Huck tells him the story about how he faked his murder. Jim relates that he overhead Miss Watson telling the widow that she was going to sell him down the river for a good sum of money. To avoid being sold, Jim ran away, and has been hiding out on Jackson's island.

Jim starts to tell Huck about various superstitious signs which the slaves watch out for. When some birds go hopping along the ground, stopping every few feet, Jim comments that means it will rain soon. He also tells Huck a story about how he lost a large sum of money, fourteen dollars at the time, by speculating. First, Jim bought a cow that died, and then invested with another slave who was setting up a "bank." Unfortunately, the bank lost all its money and poor Jim had nothing left.

Chapter 9

Jim and Huck explore the island together and discover a cavern atop a hill in the middle of the island. They paddle their canoe to the base of the hill and then haul their equipment into the cave in order to keep it dry. The storm Jim predicted arrives that night, and the river rises for more than twelve days straight.

Huck and Jim go out on the river at night to pick up drifting logs and other objects that happen to float downstream. One night, they capture a large raft which they will later use to navigate the river after they leave the island. Later on, they see a whole house floating downstream and climb into it to salvage some of the goods. Jim finds Huck's Pap lying dead on the floor of the house, but refuses to let Huck see the man's face and does not reveal that it is Pap. Jim sees Pap was shot in the back while obviously attempting to rob the house.

Chapter 10

Huck is thrilled with all the things they managed to get from the house and tells Jim that he wishes they could have fun like that more often. Huck is also still curious about the man in the house but Jim refuses to talk about him. Huck mentions that he thought they would have bad luck after he brought a snakeskin into the cave, not great luck like what they were having. Always superstitious, Jim warns Huck that the bad luck is still coming.

Three days later, Huck tries to play a trick on Jim by leaving a curled up dead rattlesnake under Jim's blanket. But when Jim crawls into the bed he gets bitten in the ankle by the snake's mate. Huck kills the mate and sheepishly carries both snakes far away from the cave, embarrassed by the results of his behavior. Jim takes the jug of Pap's whiskey and drinks himself into a drunken stupor to avoid feeling the pain of his swollen leg. It takes Jim four entire days to recover from the bite and Huck vows to never touch a snakeskin with his hands again.

In order to catch up on what is happening in the town, Huck dresses up as a girl and goes to the village. He stops at a house where he sees a woman knitting. Since she is new to the town, Huck figures he can talk to her without being recognized.

Analysis

These five chapters reveal a great deal about Huck as a person. Huck emerges as a vibrant character who fights powerfully for his life. Huck's capture and escape from Pap demonstrate his genius for innovation, as does his ability to live alone on Jackson's Island. Huck does not need anyone's help to survive, and the only indication that he is not completely happy is his comment that he sometimes gets lonely.

Huck's personality is quite uniquely established throughout these chapters. He exhibits humility in that he constantly underplays his brilliant ideas. Thus, when he fakes his death, he says that even Tom Sawyer would have been proud of the charade, indicating that Tom would have been able to fake it better but that it was a good enough to earn some praise. The innocent side of Huck is also revealed in his encounter with Jim. Jim swears him to secrecy before revealing that he has run away from Miss Watson. Huck is immediately faced with the responsibility of protecting Jim or telling the town the truth. He chooses to stay with Jim because, as a young boy who has lived outside of main stream society for quite some time, he still lacks the prejudices of the older folks in his town. This youthfulness is reinforced by the image of Huck dressing up as a girl at the end of Chapter 10.

The strength of character that leads Huck to refuse to reveal Jim at this juncture of the novel is tested many times during the course of their travels. In a sense, it is Huck's desperate need to not be alone anymore that overcomes his fear of damnation for not turning in a runaway slave. While Tom Sawyer may be his best friend as a playmate, Huck seeks someone who will care about him as a person rather than as a simple play friend. While it is not at all clear that Jim will be able to assume this role, early indications lean towards the development of this relationship as Jim works to get Huck safely inside the cave and out of the rain.

Jim's motive for keeping Pap's death from Huck is unclear. Jim could simply be trying to protect Huck's feelings, but there is also very likely a selfish motive. Jim has just revealed to Huck that he ran away from the widow. Were he to tell Huck that Pap died, there would be no reason for Huck to remain with Jim on the island. Jim fears that Huck might at some point return to town and tell people where he is hiding. Thus, for Jim, it is a life and death decision whether or not to inform Huck of Pap's death.

Summary and Analysis of Chapter 11 to Chapter 15

Chapter 11

Dressed as a girl, Huck knocks on the door of the house. The woman lets him in, believing him to be a young girl. Huck inquires about the area, and the woman talks for over an hour about her problems. She finally gets to the news about Jim and Huck and tells him that there is a three hundred dollar bounty for capturing Jim. Apparently some of the townspeople believe that Jim killed Huck and ran away, while other people believe that Pap killed Huck. She tells Huck that she personally believes Jim is hiding out on Jackson's Island.

Huck becomes nervous at this news and picks up a needle and thread. He does such a poor job of threading the needle that the woman gets suspicious of his gender. Without Huck knowing he is being tested, the woman has him throw a piece of lead at a rat in order to judge his aim. Afterwards, she reveals where Huck went wrong with his "girl" behavior and asks him what his real name is, telling him to be honest. Huck cleverly pretends to be an escaped apprentice hiding in women's clothes to avoid detection.

Huck is finally able to extricate himself from the woman and immediately returns to the island. He tells Jim to grab everything and put it in the canoe. Together they shove off, after piling their belongings onto the raft, which they then tow behind them.

Chapter 12

Jim and Huck spend the next few days traveling down the river. They improve the raft by building a wigwam, which will keep them dry and warm. Each night, Huck goes into a nearby town and buys more provisions for the next day. They only travel at night to avoid being seen and questioned.

One night, during a strong storm, they see a wrecked steamboat ahead of them. Huck convinces Jim to tie the raft to the boat and climb on board. They are surprised to hear voices, which Huck goes to investigate. There are three robbers on board, two of whom have tied up the third man. Apparently the bound man had threatened to turn them all in to the state. One of the robbers wants to kill him immediately, but the other man restrains him. The two men finally decide to kill their partner by leaving him on the boat and waiting until it sinks.

At this news, Huck scrambles back to rejoin Jim. Together they discover that their raft has come untied and floated away.

Chapter 13

Having lost their raft, Huck and Jim search along the crashed ferryboat for the robbers' skiff. Just as they find it, the two robbers emerge and place the goods they have looted into the skiff. The robbers then remember that their partner still has his share of the money, so they return to steal it from him. Before they can return back to the boat, Huck and Jim jump into the skiff, cut the rope, and speed away downstream. Before morning, they manage to find their raft again and recapture it.

Huck then goes ashore and finds a ferry night–watchman. To try to save the robbers, because he feels guilty leaving them for dead, he tells the man that his family ran into the wreck while traveling downriver and that they are stuck there. The man immediately gets his ferry moving to try and save them. However, before he gets very far, the wreck floats by, having come loose and sunk even further. Huck realizes that all three men aboard the wreck have surely drowned. Disappointed, but proud of his effort, Huck paddles downriver until he meets up with Jim. Together they sink the skiff and tie up to wait for daylight.

Chapter 14

Huck and Jim spend some time relaxing and discussing various things. Huck tells Jim all about kings and other aristocratic personages, and Jim is very impressed and interested. However, when Huck mentions King Solomon, Jim starts telling him that Solomon was one of the most foolish men who ever lived. Jim comments that any man who had as many wives as Solomon would go crazy, and that the notion of chopping a child in half in order to figure out which woman is the rightful mother is plain stupid. Jim remarks that the issue was about a whole child, not a half a child, and Solomon would have shown more respect for children if he had not had so many. Huck tries to explain the moral lesson Solomon was trying to teach, but Jim hears none of it.

Next, Huck tries to explain to Jim that Frenchmen speak a different language. Jim is surprised by this and cannot understand why all men would not speak the same language. Huck tries to make the analogy that a cat and a cow do not speak the same language, so neither should an American and a Frenchman. Jim then points out that a cat and a cow are not the same species, but Frenchmen and Americans are. He concludes that Frenchmen should therefore speak the same language he does. At this point Huck gets frustrated and gives up trying to argue with Jim.

Chapter 15

Jim is hoping to reach Cairo, at the bottom of Illinois where the Ohio river merges with the Mississippi. From there, both he and Huck will be able to take a steamboat upriver and into the free states where Jim will finally be a free man.

As they approaching that section of the river, a dense fog arrives and blankets everything in a murky white. They land on the shore, but before Huck is able to tie up the raft, the raft pulls loose and starts floating downstream with Jim aboard. Huck jumps into the canoe and follows it, but soon loses sight of it in the fog. He and Jim spend several hours tracking each other by calling out, but a large island finally separates them and Huck is left all alone.

The next morning, Huck awakens and luckily manages to catch up with the raft. He finds Jim asleep and wakes him up. Jim is glad to see him, but Huck tries to play a trick on Jim by telling him that the events of the night before were just a dream. After some convincing, Jim starts to interpret the "dream." After some time, Huck finally points out the leaves and debris left from the night before, at which point Jim gets mad at Huck for playing such a mean trick on him. Huck feels terrible about what he did and apologizes to Jim.

Analysis

These chapters provide insight into Jim's character. Jim is sincere and trustworthy, but also stubborn and mature. The chapters test Jim's loyalty to Huck, and vice–versa. For the first time the novel is dealing with the issue of loyalty, which will later have a strong impact on each character's decisions.

Jim's sincerity is established in several ways. The most potent example is his joy at seeing Huck alive again after they are separated by the fog. Jim gets upset with Huck for tricking him into believing it was all a dream precisely because he had invested a great deal of emotional pain into the adventure. In this section, it becomes obvious that Jim would be willing to sacrifice a great deal to ensure Huck's safety.

The problem at this juncture of the novel is that Huck does not yet reciprocate Jim's feelings. Huck is not yet willing to sacrifice part of his life to ensure Jim's safety, and thus leads Jim from one adventure to another, be it on the wrecked steamboat or during the fog. This is important because it is Huck's loyalty to Jim that will be tested later.

The stubborn and mature side of Jim is evidenced by his arguments with Huck and his attitude towards adventures. Huck comments that once Jim gets and idea into his head it is impossible to change it, and proves this to the reader by discussing Jim's opinions of Solomon and Frenchmen. Jim's stubbornness can partially be traced to his maturity. He desperately wishes to avoid any adventures because adventures bring complications. Jim would be happiest if he were able to get to Cairo and take the steamboat upriver with no interruptions.

Twain is famous for his sense of irony, and this section contains several examples. His best use of irony concerns the three robbers on the wrecked steamboat. When Huck and Jim lose their raft, they need to steal the robbers' skiff. However, the robbers return before they can steal it. The robbers then decide that they want all of their money, including their partner's share, and thus head back into the steamboat. Huck and Jim immediately steal the skiff. The irony is two–fold: not only are the robbers "robbed," they are also condemned to die on the steamboat as a result of their greed. Huck attempts to have them rescued, but the river acts faster than he can, by dragging the wreck further and causing it to sink too far for anyone to survive. Thus, the robbers meet the fate they condemned their partner to, namely drowning.

Summary and Analysis of Chapter 16 to Chapter 20

Summary

Chapter 16

As Jim and Huck float downriver, Jim restlessly searches the riverbank for the town of Cairo. Each time Jim mentions how soon he will be free, Huck feels increasingly guilty. Huck knows that helping Jim escape is breaking the law, but Jim is also his friend. Thus, Huck is trapped in a difficult moral dilemma. After a great deal of reasoning, Huck realizes he will feel possibly even worse if he turned Jim into the authorities, and decides it would be best to let him escape.

Huck makes this decision spontaneously, when heading to shore to determine what town they are near and with the intention of reporting Jim. On his way to shore, Huck meets two white men searching for runaway slaves. The men ask him who else is on his raft and rather than telling them about Jim, Huck tells them his Pa, mother, and sister are aboard. Huck pretends to be eager for their help and tells them no one else has been willing to pull the raft to shore. At this news, the men become suspicious and finally conclude that Huck's family must have smallpox. Each man then puts a twenty dollar coin on a log and floats it over to Huck to avoid any interaction with him, but only after making him promise not to land anywhere near their town. Huck's ingenious lie fools the men and saves Jim from capture.

Huck and Jim are thrilled to have received so much extra money, which is enough for several trips up the river. They continue watching for Cairo, but are unable to locate it. After several days, both Huck and Jim begin to suspect that they passed Cairo in the fog several nights prior. The next night, Huck and Jim start to plan to use the canoe to paddle upriver. However, the canoe disappears, forcing them to continue downriver in hopes of buying a new canoe. While drifting downstream, they encounter an oncoming steamboat. Instead of getting out of their way as the steamboats usually do, the boat ploughs directly over the raft. Both Huck and Jim are forced to dive overboard. Huck emerges and grabs a piece of wood with which he paddles to the shore. Jim is nowhere to be seen. Huck is soon surrounded by dogs and stands dripping wet and immobilized.

Chapter 17

Huck knows better than to run when surrounded by dogs, and stands stock still. Within a few moments, a man calls out to him from the house telling him to be still. After several of the men in the house prepare their rifles, Huck is allowed to approach. He cautiously enters the house and when the family sees him, they immediately become friendly. Huck has happened upon the Grangerford household, which is in a drawn out and violent feud with the nearby Shepherdson family. When the Grangerford's recognize that Huck is no relation to the Shepherdson's, they welcome him with open arms.

Huck tells the family that he is an orphan named George Jackson from down south who has lost everything, and arrived at their home after falling off of a steamboat. The Grangerford's offer him a place in their home and he agrees to stay. The youngest son, Buck, is near to Huck's age and they soon become good friends.

As Huck grows acclimated to his new home, he learns that the family had a younger daughter named Emmeline who passed away several years earlier. She was a talented poet and painter, and concentrated her work on eulogies for the dead. Huck thinks Emmeline's poetry is very beautiful and wishes that he could compose some lines devoted to Emmeline, but is unable to come up with anything.

The family is quite wealthy considering their location. They own a fairly large house with nice furnishings and even have intellectual books in the parlor. Huck is happy to stay there, especially when he discovers their wonderful cooking.

Chapter 18

Huck introduces the reader to most of the Grangerford family. The father of the house is Colonel Grangerford, whom Huck describes as a powerful, well–respected and honored man. The family owns a considerable amount of land and over one hundred slaves, including a slave for each member of the household. The two eldest sons are Tom and Bob, and the youngest is Buck, with whom Huck becomes friends. There are two daughters: Miss Charlotte, who bears herself like her father, and Miss Sophia, who is timid and kind.

While out hunting one day, Huck and Buck hear a horse approaching behind them. Quickly, they run behind a bush and wait to see who arrives. Harvey Shepherdson passes by and Buck takes a shot at him, knocking off his hat. Harvey then follows the two boys into the woods but is unable to catch them. At this point, Buck explains the family feud to Huck. For over thirty years, the men in each family have been committed to killing off the men in the opposing family. No one remembers why the feud started, but several men have been killed each year.

When the Grangerford's attend church, all the men carry guns with them, and ironically listen to preaching about brotherly love. After the service and once they have all returned home, Miss Sophia pulls Huck aside and urgently asks him to return to the church and fetch her Testament, which she accidentally left there. Huck does as he is asked and finds the book, but also sees a note that has been slipped into it which reads, "half past two." Huck returns the Testament to Sophia, and promises that he did not read the note.

When Huck goes outside, he realizes that his personal slave is following him very closely, which is unusual. The slave offers to show him some water moccasins, an offer which he had extended the day before as well. Huck realizes that the slave is speaking to him in some kind of code and that something else is going on. Huck agrees to follow him and in the swamp is surprised to find Jim asleep on the ground. Jim has the raft, which he completely repaired, and is waiting for Huck to rejoin him so they can continue their trip downriver.

The next day Miss Sophia elopes with Harvey Shepherdson, and the feud is rekindled in full force. Buck's father and both his brothers are killed in an ambush, and Huck arrives at the harbor in time to see Buck and his cousin shooting at five grown men. Eventually the men manage to sneak around Buck and kill both the boys while Huck watches from a tree that he climbed in an attempt to find safety. Once the Shepherdson's have left, Huck pulls Buck and the other boy out of the river and onto dry land where he weeps and covers their faces.

Huck runs back to the house and sees that it is quite silent in the wake of the family tragedy. He goes to the swamp, finds Jim, who is glad to see that Huck lived through the massacre, and together they push the raft into the river and start floating downstream.

Chapter 19

Huck and Jim continue down the river for a few days, enjoying the fresh air and warm breezes. Huck finds a canoe and uses it to paddle up a stream about a mile in search of berries. Two men come running through the woods and beg him for help. Huck makes them cover their tracks and then all three paddle back to the river.

The two men are humbugs and frauds who were running away from townspeople who meant to tar and feather them. One man is about seventy and balding, and the other is in his thirties. The younger man specializes in printing and theater while the older man often "works" camp revivals.

The younger man then tells them that he is actually the direct descendent of the Duke of Bridgewater and therefore is a Duke. Both Huck and Jim start to treat him as royalty and cater to his every need. This makes the older man jealous and so he then tells them that he is the Dauphin, or Louis the XVII. Huck and Jim treat both men as aristocracy, although Huck comments that it is pretty obvious neither is true royalty.

Chapter 20

Huck explains to the King and Duke that he is a farmer's son who has lost his father and brother. He tells them that Jim is the last slave the family owns and that he is traveling south to Orleans to live with his Uncle Ben. Huck also says that he and Jim travel at night because they keep getting harassed by people who think Jim is a runaway slave. The Duke tells him that he will figure out a way for them to travel during the daytime.

That night, the Duke and King take over Huck and Jim's beds. A large storm causes the river to become choppy, and Huck watches for danger. Soon Jim takes over and Huck falls asleep until he is washed overboard by a large wave. Jim bursts out laughing at the sight of Huck flailing about in the water.

The next day, the King and Duke brainstorm money making schemes. The Duke decides that they should put on a play where they perform short scenes from Shakespeare and the King agrees. After dinner, they go into a nearby town to see what luck will bring them. The men find the town deserted, as everyone has gone to a revival meeting. The Duke breaks into a printer's shop and takes orders from some farmers. He collects cash and promises to print advertisements in the paper. In his final project, he makes a handbill showing a runaway slave and describing Jim. He tells the others that this handbill will make it seem as if they are taking Jim back to collect the reward.

The King goes to the revival meeting with Huck and chances upon a crowd being listening to the preacher. The people get inflamed with the spirit of repentance, and in the middle of all their crying and yelling, the King jumps up onto the stage. He tells the audience that he was once a pirate in the Indian Ocean and that their meeting made him regret the actions of his former life. The King says that he would return to the Indian Ocean to convert his former colleagues, if only he had the money to do so. Immediately, a collection is taken up and the King leaves with over eighty–seven dollars.

Analysis

These chapters focus on social commentary of the people and places along the Southern Mississippi. Each chapter introduces new characters and adventures that highlight particular prejudices or follies. Huck is also forced to play different roles as he tries to assimilate himself into each new situation. Through each of Huck's roles, the reader receives new insight into his personality and character.

Twain offers social commentary in three separate escapades in the novel. First, two slave–hunters approach Huck's raft and Huck makes them believe his smallpox ridden family is aboard. Desperate to avoid the plague, each man forks over $20 just to keep the raft away from town. While disease is a valid concern, Twain demonstrates the fear with which people treat other sick people who need assistance and support. Rather than offering to help, the two men try to buy off the family and send them elsewhere.

Second, the Grangerford and Shepherdson families participate in a violent, tragic feud. In fact, the happenings reflect a modern day Romeo and Juliet theme, as a Grangerford daughter and Shepherdson son elope, causing a familial massacre.

Ironically, the two lovers are the only ones that survive. Huck explains how civilized, wealthy and respected the Grangerford family is, but then shatters this image by detailing the feud's excessive and tragic killings. Here, Twain demonstrates the utter stupidity of even the most educated and respected families, who can destroy themselves through nonsensical behavior and excessive pride.

The last escapade in occurs when the King bilks an entire congregation out of money. His story about being a pirate and wishing to convert his brethren is laughable and silly, but at the revival meeting, everyone is so overcome by the love of God and their fellow man that they believe him and donate to his cause. With this anecdote, Twain is commenting on the gullibility of religious zealots, which is consistent with his attack on religion in the very first pages of the novel, when Huck decides that praying and heaven as described by Miss Watson as lousy alternatives to having fun. Twain's view of religion is lucidly set forth in this and other novels, and he tends to express that devotion to religion is simply a waste of time.

Throughout these chapters, Huck consistently assumes different characters and roles in order to survive and to protect Jim. At the Grangerford's, he pretends to be an orphan, to the slave–hunters he pretends to be an innocent boy living with a sick family, and to the Duke and Dauphin, he pretends to be an orphan traveling with his only slave. Each of these roles provides great insight into Huck's personality. When Buck is killed, Huck is deeply affected by the entire tragedy and even admits to crying upon pulling his friend's dead body out of the river. He wishes that he had not played a role in causing the death of so many people, and, at the same time, realizes how foolish the feud is.

Remarkably, Huck constantly pretends to be less intelligent or less capable than he really is. It is easy to forget that he is only a boy of fourteen when he and Jim are floating down the river together. But, when they meet other people, Huck's interactions are always at a lower, less mature level. For instance, he tells the slave–hunters he is too weak to drag the raft ashore by himself, when in reality he has handled the raft alone many times. When he and Buck are together, he shows far more maturity than Buck, evidenced by his restraint in matters concerning the feud. Tom Sawyer also comes across as a young child in comparison to Huck's common sense approach to life.

Huck's interaction with the Duke and the King is at first puzzling and later annoying. He and Jim both are quite aware that the two men are con artists, forcing the reader to question why they put up with them. In fact, Huck is afraid of the consequences of crossing either man. He compares the men to Pap and remarks, "I learnt that the best way to get along with his kind of people is to let them have their own way." Thus, Huck and Jim realize that rather then stir up trouble with either of the men, it is best to play along and pretend they have been duped. Jim is unhappy with the situation, commenting at the end of Chapter 20 that he would prefer it if no more kings arrived during the trip. Huck seems to be considering a way out of the situation, but is unable to come up with a good plan. Partially, Huck enjoys watching the two men at work, since their actions create more of an adventure for him.

Summary and Analysis of Chapter 21 to Chapter 25

Summary

Chapter 21

The King and Duke turn their attention to performing scenes from Shakespeare. The King learns the lines for Juliet and practices sword–fighting with the Duke in order to perform part of Richard III. The Duke decides that a great encore would be for the King to perform Hamlet's soliloquy. Unfortunately, without the text at hand, the Duke must piece the famous lines together from memory. The end result is quite different from the true soliloquy, but still contains some elements of drama.

The men stop in a nearby town and decide to set up their show. They rent the courthouse for a night and print up bills proclaiming how wonderful the performance will be. Unfortunately, a circus is also in town, but they hope people will still attend their dramatic performances.

During the day of the show a man named Boggs rides into town. He is a drunk who comes in each month and threatens to kill a man, but never actually harms anyone. This time, he is after a Colonel Sherburn, the wealthiest man in town and a storeowner. Boggs stands outside the store and screams insults at the Colonel. The Colonel comes out of his store and tells Boggs that he will put up with the insults until one o'clock and after that he will kill him if Boggs utters even one word. Boggs continues relentlessly, and at exactly 1pm, the Colonel appears and kills Boggs on the spot. At that exact moment, Boggs's daughter approaches, hoping to save her father, but she is too late. After Boggs is laid to rest, the crowd turns into a mob and concludes that Sherburn should be lynched for the killing.

Chapter 22

The crowd travels to Sherburn's store and rips down the front fence. They halt when Sherburn emerges with a shotgun and calmly stands in front of them. He lectures the mob on how pathetic they are, tells them they are being led by half of a man, Buck Harkness, and calls them all cowards. When he finishes his speech, he cocks his gun and the crowd runs off in every direction.

Huck leaves and goes to the circus which is in town until late that night, and after which the Duke and King plan to perform their show. He sneaks in and watches all the fun activities, such as the clown and showgirls. Huck then remarks that it is the best circus he has ever witnessed and the most fun.

That night, the Shakespearean show is a disaster, with only twelve people showing up and none of them staying until the end. In response, the Duke prints up some new handbills touting a show titled the Royal Nonesuch. He then cleverly adds the line, "Ladies and Children Not Admitted" and comments that if such a line does not bring an audience, then he does not know Arkansas.

Chapter 23

The Royal Nonesuch opens to a house packed with men. The Duke greets them and hypes up the audience for the King. The King emerges completely naked, covered in paint, and crawling on all fours. The audience laughs their heads off, and he is called back to do it twice more. Then the Duke thanks them all and wishes them a good night.

The men are furious that the show is so short and realize they have been "sold," or cheated. But, before they can rush the stage in protest, one man stands up and tells them that they will be the laughingstocks of the town if it ever is revealed how badly they were cheated. They all agree to leave and tout the show for being wonderful so the rest of the town can be cheated as well.

As a result, the next night's performance is also full, and the audience leaves just as angry. The third night, all the men show up, carrying rotten eggs, dead cats, and other foul items with them. The Duke pays a man to mind the door and he and Huck rush away to the raft. They immediately push out onto the river and the King emerges from the wigwam where he and Jim have been hiding all along. Together, the two con–artists made four hundred sixty–five dollars.

That night, Jim grieves over no longer being able to see his wife and children. Huck remarks that Jim cares almost as much about his family as a white person would. Jim then tells Huck a story about when he was with his daughter, Elizabeth, one day. Jim told her to shut the door and she just stood there smiling at him. Jim got mad that she did not obey and yelled at her until he finally whacked her on the side of the head for not listening to him. Ten minutes later Jim returned and his daughter still had not closed the door. She was standing in the same place, crying. At that moment, a strong wind slammed the door behind her, causing Jim to jump. However, his daughter never moved an inch. Jim realized his poor daughter had lost her hearing. Jim tells Huck that he burst out crying upon making this realization and grabbed his daughter to give her a hug. Ever since, he has felt terrible about how he treated her.

Chapter 24

To avoid tying Jim up in ropes during the day (since he has been pretending to be a runaway slave), the Duke figures out a better solution. He paints Jim in blue and makes him wear a costume. Then, he writes a sign that reads, "Sick Arab – but harmless when not out of his head." Jim is happy that he can now move around.

The King and Huck cross the river and meet a young fool waiting for the ferry to Orleans. He proceeds to tell them all about how a Peter Wilks has died, leaving his whole estate to his daughters and brothers. The two brothers have not yet arrived from England, which greatly saddened the man before he died. The King takes a keen interest in the story and gathers every detail he can.

Once he has all the details, the King gets the Duke and tells him the entire story. The two men agree to pretend to be Peter Wilks's brothers from Sheffield, England. Together, with Huck acting as a servant, they get a steamboat to take them to the town and drop them off. Their ploy works perfectly and when they hear that Peter is dead, both men put up a huge cry and lament. Huck remarks that, "It was enough to make a body ashamed of the human race."

Chapter 25

The two con artists are taken by the crowd that greeted them upon arrival to visit the family, which consists of three orphaned girls: Mary Jane, Susan, and Joanna. Everyone exchanges hugs and cries, and then the King and Duke go to view the coffin. The two men burst out crying again, and finally the King makes a speech about how sad the whole situation is. They finish off by kissing all the women on the forehead and acting heartbroken. Huck comments that the whole scene is "disgusting."

The King and Duke discover they have received the bulk of the estate holdings as well as three thousand dollars cash. The three girls have also received three thousand dollars and the house they live in. Wilks's will tells them where in the cellar to find the cash, and the two men go downstairs and find it. The King and Duke count the money and come up four hundred and fifteen dollars short. To alleviate any suspicion, they add the money they made from the Royal Nonesuch to the pile. Then, to permanently win the town over to their side, they graciously give their share of the money to the three girls, knowing they can steal it back at anytime.

The King gives a speech and foolishly digresses. A Doctor Robinson enters the crowd, hears the King and laughs heartily, calling the King a fraud because his British accent is such a bad imitation. The townspeople rally around the King, who has been so generous, and defend him. The Doctor warns Mary Jane directly, but in response, she hands the bag of money to the King and tells him to invest it for her. The doctor warns them one final time of the mistakes they are making, and then departs.

Analysis

In these chapters, Twain again provides commentary on human nature and presents a scathing portrayal of society. Twain's 'version' of Shakespeare, Boggs's death, Jim's feelings about his family, and the Royal Nonesuch all seek to provoke the reader into analyzing the foolish ways of society. Huck assists in this encouragement by adding commentary that brings Twain's critiques into sharper focus.

The use of Shakespeare is at once funny and tragic. In describing the butchered Hamlet's soliloquy, it is immediately obvious that the Duke has muddled the lines. Moreover, the vision of the King, with his white hair and whiskers, playing fair Juliet makes even more of a mockery of the plays.

Boggs's death focuses the reader's attention on a much more serious aspect of the society. Boggs is shot to death in front of a crowd of people, including his daughter. The disrespect Boggs showed to Colonel Sherburn hardly justifies murder. Twain further derides the society for is cowardly actions, as the mob ready to lynch Sherburn is easily manipulated and succumbs to cowardice.

Twain also makes several pointed comments about the general attitude towards blacks when Jim discusses his family. Huck comments that he is surprised to find that Jim is almost as concerned about his family as a white person. This prevailing attitude, often invoked to justify breaking up slave families, is something Huck is beginning to overcome. Jim's touching story about his daughter Elizabeth, in which he hits her for not obeying him, is a powerful indication to Huck that Jim is in fact more concerned about his children than Huck's father ever was about him.

The Royal Nonesuch is perhaps Twain's most brilliant philosophical creation, a show in which the audience sees exactly what it pays for: nothing. Not only does the title accurately describe the show, but Twain cleverly has the Duke and King add the line, "Ladies and Children Not Admitted." Thus the show comments on human nature, namely that we cannot imagine a show being about nothing, even when the very title states it. The men are further fooled into thinking the Nonesuch must be some great, sexual thing, since their wives are excluded. Moreover, to avoid embarrassment, the duped men then talk up the show to their friends. Again, Twain gives a scathing review of his fellow citizens by demonstrating how fragile human egos are. The final showing, which truly is non–existent since the Duke and King run off before it starts, is a coup for the two conmen, who once again give the citizens exactly what they pay for. One wonders whether it is possible to hold them guilty of a crime, considering that in reality, they were honest about the content of the show.

However, the conmen's next adventure proves them highly despicable individuals. The Duke and King sink even lower in their abuse of human gullibility and nature by pretending to be the uncles of three orphaned girls in order to steal their inheritance. Huck's views on this scheme are clear, as he calls the King and Duke "disgusting" and remarks that he is "ashamed of the human race."

These chapters offer us a great deal of new insight into Huck Finn. He is obviously maturing in his views, as evidenced by his belief that black and white people are not so different. He is also changing from a boy who lacks firm morals to a man with a commitment to values. Thus, his commentary is no longer merely descriptive, but increasingly evaluative. It is becoming obvious that Huck will soon not be content to stand aside and let things slide past, as the metaphor of gliding down the river suggests. Instead, Huck will take a stand and assert himself as an individual. Huck's attitudes will eventually bear fruit in his actions, marking the final step in his journey towards maturity.

Summary and Analysis of Chapter 26 to Chapter 30

Summary

Chapter 26

The night of the doctor's warning, Joanna and Huck eat together, since they are the youngest two people present. She asks him all about England, and Huck lies to her in order to sound knowledgeable. She catches him in several of the lies, and Huck keeps pretending to choke on a chicken bone in order to think of a way out. Mary Jane overhears Joanna telling Huck that she does not believe him and makes Joanna apologize to Huck for being so rude. Huck decides he cannot let the King and Duke steal the money from these extremely kind girls.

Huck goes to the King's room and hides when he hears the Duke and King approaching. The conmen debate whether they should leave now that suspicion has been raised or wait until the rest of the property is sold off. They choose to stay and hide their money in the straw tick mattress. Huck steals the money immediately and waits until it is safe to slip downstairs to hide it.

Chapter 27

Huck is afraid he will be caught with the stolen money, so he hides it inside Peter Wilks's coffin. That day, the funeral service is held, and is interrupted by loud barking from a dog locked in the cellar. The undertaker goes to silence the dog, returns, and tells the audience the dog caught a rat. Huck remarks that the service was long and tiresome, but is relieved when Peter Wilks and the money are finally buried.

The King and Duke immediately begin selling everything they can, including the slave family owned by the household. To sell the slaves faster, they break up the family. The girls are extremely upset by this insensitivity. Many of the townspeople also expressed disapproval, but the men are not swayed.

On the day of the auction, the King realizes the money is gone. He questions Huck, who cleverly blames the slaves who were sold. Both the Duke and King feel extremely foolish for selling the slaves at such low prices considering all their money is now lost.

Chapter 28

Later that morning, Huck sees Mary Jane sitting on her floor, crying while packing to go to England with her uncles. Mary Jane explains that she is upset about the slaves being so mistreated, and Huck blurts out that they will be together again in two weeks at the most, knowing the Duke and King will abandon the town. When he realizes he has slipped, he decides to tell her everything. She becomes furious as he relates the story, and when Huck finishes, she calls the King a "brute."

Huck makes Mary Jane leave the house and stay with a friend across the river. Before she leaves, he writes down where the money is located so she will be able to find it later on. Huck is afraid that if Mary Jane stays at the house, her face will give away Huck's indiscretion. Huck tells her sisters that she is across the river trying to stir up interest in buying the house. After telling this part of the story to the reader, Huck remarks that he has never forgotten Mary Jane and still thinks she is one of the most beautiful girls he has ever met.

The auction occurs that afternoon and the King works hard to sell every last thing. In the middle of the auction, a steamboat lands, and two men claiming to be the real heirs to the Wilks's fortune disembark. As they approach the crowd, Huck notices that the elder man is speaking, and that the younger man's right arm is in a sling.

Chapter 29

The new heirs claim to have lost their baggage and are therefore unable to prove their identity. The King and Duke continue pretending to be the real heirs. Both groups are taken to the tavern where Levi Bell and Dr. Robinson grill them for information.

The first information revealed is that the Wilks money has been stolen, which looks bad for the King and Duke. However, they blame it on the slaves and continue pretending. The lawyer, Levi Bell, manages to get all three men to write a line for him. He pulls out some old letters and examines the handwriting, only to discover that none of three men had written the letters to Peter Wilks. The real Harvey Wilks explains that his brother had transcribed all his letters because his handwriting is so poor. Unfortunately, since his brother has a broken arm, he cannot write and therefore they cannot prove their case.

Harvey Wilks then remembers that his deceased brother had his initials tattooed on his chest and challenges the King to tell him what was on Peter's chest, assuming that the men who had laid his brother out would have seen the mark and will be able to determine who is lying. Refusing to give up, the King continues pretending and tells them Peter had a blue arrow tattooed on his chest. The men who laid out Peter Wilks cannot remember seeing anything, and thus they are forced to exhume the body.

The entire town travels to the gravesite. When they finally unearth and open the casket, they discover the gold Huck has hidden there. Immediately, the men holding the King and Duke let go to get a look at the money. At this opportunity, Huck, the King, and the Duke run to the river as fast as they can. Huck gets to the raft and takes off down the river, hoping to escape the two men. When the Duke and King catch up to him in a little skiff, he almost starts to cry.

Chapter 30

After the King boards the raft, he grabs Huck, shakes him, and yells at him for trying to get away and for escaping without waiting. The Duke finally intervenes and calls the King an "old idiot," asking, "Did you enquire for him when you got loose?"

Next, the King and Duke get into an argument about the money and start accusing each other of stealing the cash and hiding it, especially since they had added the proceeds of the Royal Nonesuch to the pot. The Duke finally physically attacks the King and forces him say that he took the money. Next, both men get drunk, but Huck notices the King never again admits to taking the money and rather denies it at every opportunity.

Analysis

These chapters mark Huck's first moments of maturity. Up until this point, he followed the authority of those around him, such as Pap, the Widow, Miss Watson, Judge Thatcher, and the King and Duke. The moment Huck decides to steal the money, he breaks free of this authority. For the first time, Huck acts on his convictions and morals to help other people, rather than simply acting on his personal desires.

Huck's interaction with Mary Jane also highlights an emerging aspect of his growth, namely an interest in women. In *The Adventures of Tom Sawyer*, Huck viewed girls as nothing more than an annoyance and did not believe they were to be taken seriously. Here, in contrast, Huck calls Mary Jane beautiful, and comments that when he saw her light a candle in the window, his "heart swelled up sudden, like to burst."

In addition, it is notable that Huck is desperate to escape the King and the Duke by the end of the Wilks ordeal. Huck is not simply scared of them (when he first meets them he compares them to his Pap), but is truly attempting to break free from the authority and control that they hold over him.

Interestingly, Jim is not a part of these scenes. However, we do meet a slave family torn apart by the King and Duke. Twain places this scene directly after Jim's emotionally charged story of his daughter's hearing loss and their subsequent separation, a very purposeful choice. Twain was vehemently opposed to slavery, and abhorred this aspect of the institution. Thus, Twain is trying to subconsciously influence his reader every step of the way by directing their emotions towards sympathy for the slaves. In observing the fate of this slave family, the reader begins to more powerfully grasp Jim's reasons for running away.

Summary and Analysis of Chapter 31 to Chapter 35

Summary

Chapter 31

The Duke and King spend a few days plotting how to recover their fortunes. Soon, they reach a village named Pikesville. The King leaves and tells the Duke and Huck to follow him if he does not return by midday. After he fails to reappear, they go to find him, leaving Jim with the raft. Huck and the Duke search for quite some time, and finally find the King in a tavern. Soon, both the Duke and King are drunk.

Huck sees his chance and runs straight back to the raft, but when he arrives Jim is gone. A young man on the road tells him Jim, a runaway slave, was just captured and sold to the Phelps family, down the road. Huck realizes that in an effort to make some money, the King had snuck back to the raft while he and the Duke had been searching for him, took Jim, sold him for forty dollars, and returned to the town to drink.

Huck sits down and contemplates his next move. He is torn between his friendship for Jim and his belief that helping a runaway slave is a sin. Huck finally writes a letter to Miss Watson explaining where Jim is. Not quite satisfied, he thinks about it some more, and, in one of the most dramatic scenes in the novel, rips apart the letter saying, "All right, then, I'll go to hell!"

Huck starts walking to the Phelps's farm, but encounters the Duke along the way. The Duke is posting advertisements for the Royal Nonesuch, which the two men are planning to perform again. When he sees Huck, the Duke gets extremely nasty and is afraid Huck will warn the townspeople. Next, he lies to Huck and tells him Jim was sold to a farm several days away and threatens Huck in order to keep him silent. Huck promises not to say a word, and hopes he will never have to deal with men such as the Duke and King ever again.

Chapter 32

Huck decides to trust his luck, and walks directly up to the front door of the Phelps's farm. He is quickly surrounded by about fifteen hound dogs, which scatter when a large black woman chases them away. Aunt Sally emerges and hugs Huck, saying "It's you, at last! – ain't it?" Entirely surprised, Huck merely mutters "yes'm."

Aunt Sally drags Huck into the house and starts to ask him why he is so late. Not sure how to respond, Huck says the steamboat blew a cylinder. The woman asks if anyone was hurt, to which Huck replies, "No'm, killed a nigger." Before he has a chance to answer any more questions, Silas Phelps returns home after picking up his nephew at the wharf. Aunt Sally hides Huck, pretends he is not there, then drags him out and surprises Silas. Silas does not recognize Huck until Aunt Sally announces, "It's Tom Sawyer!" Huck nearly faints from joy when he hears his friend's name and realizes Aunt Sally is Tom's aunt.

Over the next two hours, Huck tells the family all about the Sawyer's and entertains them with stories. Soon, he hears a steamboat coming down the river, and realizes Tom is probably on the boat, since the family was expecting him. Eager to meet his friend and keep himself safe, Huck tells Aunt Sally and Silas that he must return to town to fetch his baggage, quickly explaining they need not accompany him.

Chapter 33

Huck meets Tom Sawyer on the road and stops his carriage. Tom is frightened, thinking Huck is a ghost, but Huck reassures him and they settle down to catch up. Huck tells Tom what has happened at the Phelps's, and Tom thinks about how they should proceed. He tells Huck to return to the farm with his suitcase, while Tom returns to town and begins his trip to the Phelps's again.

Huck arrives back at the Phelps house, and soon thereafter, Tom arrives. The family is excited because they do not get very many visitors, so they make Tom welcome. Tom makes up a story about his hometown and then suddenly and impudently kisses Aunt Sally right on the mouth. Shocked at his behavior, she nearly hits him over the head with her spinning stick, until Tom reveals that he is Sid Sawyer, Tom's brother.

Next, Silas tells the family that their new slave Jim warned him about the Royal Nonesuch, and that he took it upon himself to inform the rest of the town. Silas figures the two cheats Jim spoke of will be ridden out of town that night. In a last minute attempt to warn the Duke and King, Huck and Tom climb out of their windows, but they are too late. They see the two men being paraded through the street covered in tar and feathers. Observing the scene, Huck remarks that human beings can be awfully cruel to one another.

Chapter 34

Tom and Huck brainstorm ways to break Jim out of his prison. Huck plans to get the raft, steal the key to the padlock, unlock the door and then float down the river some more. Tom claims that plan is too simple and would work too well. Tom's plan is much more elaborate and stylish, and takes a great deal longer to implement.

The boys go to the hut where Jim is being kept and search around. Finally, Tom decides that the best way, or at least the way that will take the longest, is to dig a hole for Jim to climb out of. The next day, he and Huck follow the black man who is delivering Jim's food. Jim recognizes Huck and Tom and calls them by name, but both boys pretend not to hear. When he has a chance, Tom tells Jim that they are going to dig him out. Jim is so happy he grabs Tom's hand and shakes it.

Chapter 35

To create as fantastical a story and game as possible, Tom tries to determine how to make Jim into a real prisoner before his daring escape. He decides that he and Huck will have to saw off the leg of Jim's bed in order to free the chain, send him a knotted ladder made of sheets, give him a shirt to keep a journal on, and get him some tin plates to write messages on and throw out the window. To top it off, Tom tells Huck that they will use case–knives to dig Jim out, rather than the much quicker and more appropriate picks and shovels.

Analysis

This section of the novel dramatically forces Huck to finally decide what he believes about slavery, and, as such, solidify his own morality. The most powerful scene occurs when Huck writes a letter to Miss Watson explaining where Jim is, only to tear it up, accept his fate no matter what the consequence of following his conscience, and set out to free Jim. Huck is willing to sacrifice his soul for Jim's freedom, showing a tremendous amount of personal growth. This scene indicates how his relationship with Jim has changed over the course of the journey downriver, from companion, to respected friend, to the only family Huck will acknowledge. Huck decides to free Jim after remembering all the times Jim protected and cared for him, something which no one else has ever done for Huck.

Therefore, there is bitter irony in Huck's story about the steamship cylinder exploding. Huck concocts the tale as an excuse for arriving in town so much later than expected, and when asked if anyone was hurt, he replies "No'm, killed a nigger." Aunt Sally is relieved to hear that no white people where hurt or killed, and does not care that a black person died. In the beginning of the book, the reader could easily attribute racist attitudes to the culture and time, forgiving the speaker for his or her ignorance, but after being introduced to Jim, the reader is unable to maintain that distance. Thus, it is surprising to hear Huck make such a racist and hypocritical off handed comment, but perhaps he is simply speaking in a way he thinks Aunt Sally would relate.

In this section, Twain's writing style also returns to that of *The Adventures of Tom Sawyer*. Tom's return signifies that logical thinking will disappear, and an excessive sense of adventure and fantasy will take over. Huck quickly takes a backseat when Tom's unlimited creativity is released upon the Phelps home.

Tom's willingness to steal a slave is surprising to Huck. It is somewhat of a surprise to the reader too, considering the long moral journey Huck experience to decide he would risk hell for his friend. Thus, Huck questions Tom's motives, and finally concludes it is simply Tom's juvenile love for adventure that is spurring him on. The reader must recognize this as a false assumption. Tom has never committed a true crime with serious moral repercussions, and is thus unlikely to do so now. As the reader discovers in later chapters, Tom knows that Jim is already free, although Jim is unaware. Therefore, Tom knows he and Huck aren't breaking the law, but keeps this information from Huck so he will continue to play the prisoner game.

Summary and Analysis of Chapter 36 to Chapter 40

Summary

Chapter 36

The next night, Tom and Huck sneak out and start digging with their case knives. They tire soon and their hands quickly develop blisters, but it seems they haven't accomplished anything. Tom finally sighs and agrees to use a pick and shovel, but only as long as they pretend to be using case knives. Huck agrees and tells Tom his head is getting "leveler" all the time.

The next day, they steal some tin plates and a brass candlestick for Jim to write with. They also finish digging the hole and make it possible for Jim to crawl out. Jim wants to escape immediately, but Tom then tells Jim all about the little things he needs to do first, including writing in blood, throwing the tin plates out of the hut, etc. Jim thinks all of these ideas are a little crazy, but agrees to do it.

Tom then convinces the man who brings Jim his food that Jim is bewitched and offers to heal him by baking a pie, in which he plans to conceal the sheet ladder.

Chapter 37

Aunt Sally notices that she has lost a sheet, a shirt, six candles, a spoon and a brass candlestick. Very confused by the strange disappearances, she becomes absolutely livid. Aunt Sally yells at poor Silas, who eventually discovers the missing spoon in his pocket, where Tom had placed it. He looks ashamed and promises her he has no idea how the spoon got into his pocket. Aunt Sally then yells at everyone to get away from her and let her get some peace and quiet.

Tom decides that the only way to steal back the spoon is to confuse his poor Aunt Sally even further. Tom has Huck hide one of spoons while Aunt Sally counts them, and then Huck puts it back when Aunt Sally counts again. By the time she has finished counting, Aunt Sally has no idea exactly how many spoons she has, and Tom is able to take one without any more trouble. Tom then does the same thing with the sheet, by stealing one out of her closet and putting it on the clothesline, only to remove it the next day.

The boys bake Jim a witches pie, in which they hide the rope. It takes them several hours to get it right because the pie is so large, but they finally succeed. The man who normally takes Jim his food takes the pie in to him, and Jim happily removes the rope.

Chapter 38

Tom designs a coat–of–arms for Jim to inscribe on the walls so as to permanently leave his mark on the prison cell. Next, Tom works out three mournful inscriptions and tells Jim he must carve them into a rock. Huck and Tom go to fetch an old grindstone for Jim to use as his rock, but it is too heavy for them to carry, so they are forced to allow Jim to leave his "prison" and come help them. Jim rolls the rock into the hut and sets to work on the inscriptions.

Tom decides that Jim needs some cell companions, such as snakes and spiders. He tells Jim that he and Huck will find some for him, but Jim is vehemently opposed to the idea. Tom then tries to convince Jim to get a flower so he can water it with his tears. Jim replies that the flower would not last very long. Tom finally gets frustrated, and gives up for the night.

Chapter 39

Huck and Tom spend the next day catching creatures to live with Jim in his cell. They first gather about fifteen rats, but Aunt Sally's son frees them by accident and both Tom and Huck receive beatings for bringing rats into her house. Determined, the boys catch another fifteen rats, along with some spiders, caterpillars, frogs, and bugs. At the end of the day they gather some garter snakes and put them in a bag, but after dinner they discover all the snakes escaped in the house as well. Huck remarks that there was no shortage of snakes in the house for quite a while after that.

Uncle Silas decides to start advertising Jim as a runaway slave in some of the local newspapers because he has failed to receive a reply to his earlier letters. Since the plantation to which he wrote never existed, it makes sense that he never received a reply. Tom figures out how to stop Silas, by planting anonymous letters that warn him off this plan of action. Tom and Huck first plant a letter reading, "Beware. Trouble is brewing. Keep a sharp lookout." The next night the boys tack up a letter containing a skull and crossbones, which they follow with a picture of a coffin.

Tom plans a final coup by drafting a longer letter. Pretending to be a member of a gang of robbers who are planning to steal Jim from the family, he warns them that the gang will be coming late at night from the north to get Jim. The family is terribly frightened and does not know what to do.

Chapter 40

The letter has a strong effect, and over fifteen armed farmers are sitting in the house waiting for the robbers to come during the night of the escape. Huck is frightened for their safety when he slips out the window and tells Tom they must leave immediately or they will be shot. Tom gets very excited when he hears about how many people came to catch them.

As Tom, Huck and Jim start to move away from the hut, Tom gets caught on the fence and his britches rip quite loudly. All three start to run, and the farmers shoot after them. When they get to a dark area, Huck, Jim, and Tom hide behind a bush and let the whole pack of farmers and dogs run past them.

Once safe, they proceed to where the raft is hidden and Tom tells Jim he is a free man again, and that he will always be a free man from now on. Jim thanks him and tells him it was a great escape plan. Tom then shows them where he got a bullet in the leg, but Jim is worried for Tom's health. Jim rips up one of the Duke's old shirts and ties up the leg with it.

Jim tells Tom that he is not going to move until they get a doctor there and make sure he is safe. Tom gets mad at both of them and yells, but Huck ignores him and gets the canoe ready to go to town. Tom makes him promise to blindfold the doctor before bringing him back to their hiding place.

Analysis

Most of the action in these chapters mirror Tom's humorous adventures in *The Adventures of Tom Sawyer*. There is a serious anti–slavery undercurrent, as Jim and Huck are concerned only with breaking Jim out of slavery, and don't understand that for Tom, this is all just a game.

In truth, these chapters provide a conclusion to Huck and Jim's journey downriver. Huck is reunited with Tom, and it is becoming clear that there will be happy ending for all. We have now departed from Huck's story and reentered the story of Tom and Huck, which is where the novel began. Once again, Tom is making the decisions, while Huck merely plays along, and Jim simply accepts. Interestingly, Tom is still the same boy he was when the reader last saw him in the earliest chapters of the novel. However, Huck has developed into a more mature, morally sound individual. Huck always thought Tom's make believe adventures were not worth the time or effort Tom put into them. But, here, he believes they are truly setting Jim free, and releasing him from the bonds of slavery. For Huck, this is one of the most serious and risky actions he has ever undertaken, but for Tom, it is all just a game.

Summary and Analysis of Chapter 41 to Chapter 43

Chapter 41

Huck returns to town and finds a doctor. Instead of allowing Huck to come along, the doctor makes Huck tell him where the raft is and takes the canoe out alone to find Tom and Jim. Huck falls asleep on a woodpile while waiting for him to return. When he wakes up, he is told the doctor has not yet returned.

Huck soon sees Silas, who is very glad Huck is not hurt. Together, they go to the post office, and Silas asks where Sid is. Huck makes up a story about Sid taking off to gather news about the events of the night. When they return home, Aunt Sally makes a fuss over Huck, but is glad he has returned.

A large gathering is held at the house, and the women discuss how they think Jim must have been crazy due to Jim's grindstone inscriptions and the tools found in his hut, all of which Huck and Tom actually crafted.

Aunt Sally is worried about Sid's whereabouts. Huck tells her the same tale he told Uncle Silas, but it does not set her mind at ease. During the night, Huck sneaks out several times and each time sees her sitting with a lit candle on the front porch, waiting for Sid's return. Huck feels very sorry for her and wishes he could tell her everything.

Chapter 42

The next day, the doctor appears, bringing Tom on a stretcher and Jim in chains. Tom is comatose due to a fever from the bullet wound, but is still alive. Aunt Sally takes him inside and immediately starts to care for him. Tom improves rapidly and is almost completely better by the next day.

Huck goes into the bedroom to sit with Tom and see how he is doing. Aunt Sally walks in as well and while both of them are sitting there, Tom wakes up. He immediately starts to tell Aunt Sally about everything the two of them did and how they managed to help Jim escape. Aunt Sally cannot believe they were creating all of the trouble around her house.

When Tom hears that Jim has been recaptured he shouts at them that they cannot chain Jim up anymore. He tells them that Jim has been free ever since Miss Watson died and freed him in her will. Apparently Miss Watson was so ashamed about planning to sell Jim that she felt it best to set him free.

At that moment Aunt Polly, Aunt Sally's sister, appears. Aunt Sally is so surprised that she rushes over to her sister to give her a hug. Aunt Polly proceeds to tell Aunt Sally that the boys masquerading as Tom and Sid are actually Huck and Tom. Embarrassed, the boys look quite sheepish. Aunt Polly only gets angry when she discovers that Tom has been stealing and hiding her letters. She also explains to Aunt Sally that in regards to Jim, Tom is correct. Miss Watson freed Jim in her will.

Chapter 43

Tom tells Huck he had planned for them to run all the way to the mouth of the Mississippi if they had managed to escape unharmed. Jim gets a positive reception in the house because of how well he cared for Tom when he was sick. Tom, feeling slightly guilty, gives Jim forty dollars for putting up with them the entire time and for being such a good prisoner. Jim turns to Huck and tells him he was right about being a rich man one day.

Huck asks about his six thousand dollars, assuming Pap managed to take it all. However, Tom explains that Pap was never seen again after Huck disappeared. Finally, Jim reveals that the man he and Huck found dead in the floating house was in fact Pap, but Jim had not wanted Huck to see him.

Huck ends the novel by announcing that Aunt Sally wants to adopt him now, so he needs to start planning on heading west since he tried to be civilized once before, and did not like it.

Analysis

There are several key facts revealed in the final chapters that influence how the reader views each character. Tom announces that Jim is free, which reveals why Tom was willing to help Huck in what Huck thought was a true crime. Since Jim was already a free man, Tom was not breaking any laws and therefore thought the entire ordeal was a great adventure.

The second major revelation is that Pap is dead. Jim has known this for most of the journey, in fact since leaving Jackson's Island. However, Jim's motivation for hiding this secret from Huck is unclear. Perhaps Jim felt sorry for Huck and wanted to care for him since he was now an orphan. Or, perhaps Jim knew that if Huck found out Pap was dead, he would simply have returned to town and ended his runaway journey. Without Huck, Jim would have had a far more difficult journey downriver as a lone black man and runaway slave. Having developed a strong understanding of Jim's character, it seems most likely that Jim was motivated by kindness, but a selfish desire for Huck's companionship might also have played a role.

The ending appears to leave Huck almost exactly where he started. However, Huck has changed significantly during the course of his travels. Huck's comment that he needs to head west before they try to civilize is significant, because we know that Huck can act civilized when he needs to, as he survived well in his many extended stays at Southern family estates. In the beginning of the novel, Huck is a poor, simple, uneducated boy. However, by the conclusion of novel, Huck is a crafty, intelligent, wealthy young man who simply does not care to be a part of a boring middle–class lifestyle. Huck changes profoundly in the course of this novel, struggles with powerful moral issues, risks his life for those he cares about, and thrives in the process.

In addition, the depiction of black slaves changes dramatically in the course of the novel. At first, slaves are merely background characters, carrying out chores while white characters monopolize the plot. However, this changes with the introduction of Jim, and continues to develop even when Jim leaves the plot for brief periods. Thus, the King's forced break–up of the Wilks's slave family powerfully impacts the reader, whereas before getting to know Jim, it might not have been perceived as so significant. In addition to being a story about Huck's growth and maturation, and resulting freedom from his Pap, *The Adeventures of Huckleberry Finn* is also a story about Jim's journey towards freedom. By ending the novel with Jim becoming a free man, with money to his name, Twain provides a clear social commentary about the immorality of slavery.

The Adventures of Huckleberry Finn is Twain's literary masterpiece. To create this novel he first overcame the difficulty of writing in the first person from a young boy's perspective. The novel is also a testament to the various dialects and characteristics of the southern regions. Lastly, *The Adventures of Huckleberry Finn* is a story about freedom, as it deals with physical freedom for the slaves and spiritual freedom for both Jim and Huck. Few novels have approached the success of *The Adventures of Huckleberry Finn* in combining such serious issues with Twain's characteristically delightful humor.

Suggested Essay Questions

1. Select five characters that Twain does not admire in Huck Finn. Name and describe the specific traits that each possesses that makes him or her not an admirable person.

2. Select five characters that Twain does admire. Name and discuss the specific traits that each possesses that makes him or her admirable.

3. Violence and greed are motivations of much of the action in this book. Discuss, giving at least three examples of each.

4. Mark Twain was able to find humor in situations that most people would regard as serious. Discuss and provide specific references from the novel.

5. Some critics claim that Jim is Huck's "true father." Defend or refute this statement.

6. Discuss the qualities Huck posesses which are necessary for survival on the frontier. Give specific examples from the novel.

7. What is the symbolic importance of the setting of the novel (land vs. river)?

8. What does the reader infer about Twain's attitude towared slavery and racism?

9. Discuss how the river provides freedom for Huck.

10. What is "civilization" in the mind of Huck?

11. Discuss how Huck grows as a person; what life lessons does he learn from his encounters on the river?

12. Although Mark Twain, in his introductory "notice" to the novel, denies that there is a moral or motive in the story, the work itself contradicts its author. How?

13. Discuss the role of religion in the novel.

14. Discuss Huck as an archetype hero.

15. What does Twain admire in a man and what is he contemptuous of?

16. This novel is also a satire on human weaknesses. What human traits does he satirize? Give examples for each.

17. What evidence do you find of Twain's cynicism?

18. Discuss three recurring motifs (any idea, object, feeling, color, pattern, etc. which repeats itself) in the novel. Give specifics.

19. Discuss the role of superstition in the novel. Explain how Twain criticizes superstitious beliefs and give specific examples.

20. Appearance versus reality is a major theme in Huckleberry Finn. Using specifics from the book, discuss this very prevalent theme.

21. How does Huck search for a family? What does he find and what does he learn?

22. How is Huck's trip down the river actually a passage into manhood?

23. How would you defend Huckleberry Finn against charges of being a racist novel?

24. Huckleberry Finn has been called the "Great American Novel." However, it is the sixth most frequently banned book in the United States. Discuss why this masterpiece is banned mostly in Christian academies and in all black

institutions.

25. Explain how the American Dream is or is not achieved by three characters in this novel. Begin by explaining what each character holds as his or her American Dream.

26. Discuss how Huck displays several textbook characteristics of the child of an alcoholic.

27. Analyze and trace the moral maturation of Huck Finn. Discuss the events that disgusted and depressed him, the coping skills that he learned, and his actions and the circumstances for such.

28. "Picaresque" is a word used to describe a character who comes from a low class of society, is poor, lives by his/her wits, travels, and has eposodic adventures. Using specific examples and quotes from the novel, explain how Huck is a picaresque figure.

29. A persona is an alternate name and personality uses for many different reasons. Discuss the many personas used in the novel.

30. Discuss the similarities and differences between Jim and Pap, as parents.

31. If you had to name a modern day Huck Finn who would it be?

32. Explain how Huck's loss of innocence as a boy is symbolic of America as the country moves towards the Civil War.

33. Compare and contrast Realism and Romanticism in the novel.

34. Select two of the social institutions (i.e. democracy) at which Twain pokes fun. Use specific references to show how he accomplishes this.

35. What do you think makes this novel an important record of American culture?

36. Point out the weak and strong character traits in Huck. How do his character and personality compare with those of Tom Sawyer?

37. Lionel Trilling says that Huck possesses a sense of humor. Do you think this is so? Site examples for a yes or no answer.

38. A major unifying element in the novel is illusion (pretense) vs. reality. Find examples. Explain their significance to Twain's overall themes.

39. Identify the literary techniques used by Mark Twain in Huckleberry Finn. Consider techniques such as: figures of speech, language, narrative techniques, sentence structure, diction, organization, syntax, detail, structure, imagery, irony, and tone.

40. How does Mark Twain create a humorous effect (exaggeration, irony, satire, understatement)?

41. How does Twain use satire to expose and criticize human failings?

42. Discuss Jim as a Christ figure.

43. As a way of illustrating his theme, Twain deliberately sets certain events with Huck and Jim on the river and others on the shore. Compare and contrast the major events on the river with those on the shore and develop a supportable thesis for why you think he makes the choices he does. How do these choices subtly reinforce his theme? Back up your thesis with specific quotes and detailed explanations.

44. Discuss how Twain criticises the values of Southern society by showing the difference between Huck's acquired values and his own innate sense of

goodness.

45. Discuss the theme of individual conscience verses society and how it relates to the theme of freedom in the novel.

46. Authors often use dramatic irony to define something. Describe how Mark Twain uses dramatic irony to define "freedom."

47. In some ways Huck's story is mythical but it is also an anti–myth –– a challenge to the deceits which individuals and cultures use to disguise their true natures from themselves. In the midst of this deceitful culture, Huck stands as a peculiarly honest individual. Discuss, referencing the novel.

48. Discuss the Civilized, Primitive, and Natural Man in Huck Finn.

49. Huck is born into nature, but is morally influenced by society.How does the book show Huck's development into trusting his natural morals again?

50. Discuss historical revisionism and whether Huck Finn should be part of a high school curriculm.

51. The overall American critical reaction to the publishing of The Adventures of Huck Finn in 1855 was summed up in one word: "trash". Louisa May Alcott (author of Little Women and Little Men) said, "If Mr. Clemens cannot think of anything better to tell our pure–minded lads and lassies, he had better stop writing for them." The Public Library Committee of Concord, Massachusetts excluded the book as "a dangerous moral influence on the young." Defend or refute the position that the novel is indeed "trash" with evidence from the text to support your claim.

52. Compare and contrast Rule of the Bone by Russell Banks with Huckleberry Finn.

53. Twain's writings were directly affected by him growing up in Hannibal. How did Twain write about himself through the characters Huck Finn and Tom Sawyer as well as through many others?

Irony

Dramatic

Chapter 9

> "When we was ready to shove off we was a quarter of a mile
> below the island, and it was pretty broad day; so I made Jim lay
> down in the canoe and cover up with a quilt, because if he set up
> people could tell he was a nigger a good ways off." –Pg. 58

Here, Huck incorrectly assumes that people can distinguish a black person from a
white person from a significant distance. At this point, he still holds the belief that
blacks are essentially different from whites.

Chapter 10

> "His foot swelled up pretty big, and so did his leg; but by and by
> the drunk begun to come, and so I judged he was all right; but I'd
> druther been bit with a snake than pap's whisky."

Huck is inadvertently demonstrating how little he cares for his Pap, by saying he'd
rather be bitten by a snake than be drunk off Pap's whisky.

Chapter 14

> "…he judged it was all up with him anyway it could be fixed; for if
> he didn't get saved he would get drownded; and if he did get saved,
> whoever saved him would send him back home so as to get the
> reward, and then Miss Watson would sell him South, sure. Well,
> he was right; he was most always right; he had an uncommon level
> head for a nigger." –Pg. 81

Raised in Southern slave owning society, Huck joins in the common belief that
blacks are less intelligent than whites. Therefore, he seems astonished that Jim has
such a "level head".

Chapter 17

> 'I bet you can't spell my name,' says I.
>
> 'I bet you what you dare I can', says he.
>
> 'All right,' says I, 'go ahead.'

'G–e–o–r–g–e J–a–x–o–n—there now,' he says.

'Well,' says I, 'you done it, but I didn't think you could.

It ain't no slouch of a name to spell—right off without studying.'

I set down, private, because somebody might want me to spell it next, and so I wanted to be handy with it and rattle it off like I was used to it." –Pg. 103

Ironically, Buck misspells Huck's pseudonym, and Huck memorizes the misspelling in case someone asks him about it.

Chapter 18

"Each person had their own nigger to wait on them—Buck too. My nigger had a monstrous easy time, because I warn't used to having anybody do anything for me, but Buck's was on the jump most of the time." –Pg. 109

Most people in Huck's place would have loved having a personal servant, but Huck is uncomfortable, and refuses to take advantage of the man assigned to him. Although he does adhere to aspects of racism ingrained in him due to his upbringing, he has more respect for blacks than most Southerners of the time.

Chapter 19

…"we was always naked, day and night, whenever the mosquitoes would let us—the new clothes Buck's folks made for me was too good to be comfortable, and besides I didn't go much on clothes, nohow." –Pg. 121

Again, Huck is offered the chance to assimilate with mainstream society, but eschews it in favor of comfortable, free living.

Chapter 22

"The minute he was on, the horse begun to rip and tear and jump and cavort around…It warn't funny to me, though; I was all of a tremble to see his danger." –Pg. 149

Huck is the only person in the crowd with the sense to worry about the safety of the drunkard on the horse. Even though he's a runaway, Huck is morally superior and more aware than the common people who surround him in this scene.

Chapter 24

"He said it was a sight better than lying tied a couple of years
every day, and trembling all over every time there was a sound."
–Pg. 157

Jim is wearing clothes for which he is ridiculed as a freak, but to him, ridicule is far
better than being tied up and left alone.

Chapter 25

"…every woman, nearly, went up to the girls, without saying a
word, and kissed them, solemn, on the forehead, and then put their
hand on their head, and looked up towards the sky, with the tears
running down, and then busted out and went off sobbing and
swabbing, and give the next woman a show. I never see anything
so disgusting." –Pg. 163

Huck seriously dislikes fake and contrived people, and the act these women are
putting on frustrates him to no end. Although they are weeping, Huck is actually a
more sensitive and honest person.

Chapter 28

"I says to myself, I reckon a body that ups and tells the truth when
he is in a tight place is taking considerable many resks, though I
ain't had no experience, and can't say for certain; but it looks so to
me, anyway…" –Pg. 184

Here, Huck is honest about his dishonesty.

Situational

Chapter 11

"'Some think old Finn done it himself… But before night they
changed around and judged it was done by a runaway nigger
named Jim.'" –Pg. 83

In this quote, Twain demonstrates that when crimes occurred, blacks were
immediately blamed before whites.

Chapter 15

"We could sell the raft and get on a steamboat and go way up the
Ohio amongst the free states, and then be out of trouble." –Pg. 85

Huck believes his and Jim's lives will be perfect if they are able to get down the river, but in reality, there's no way of knowing whether they might end up worse off than when they started.

Chapter 16

> "There warn't nothing to do now but to look out sharp for the town, and not pass it without seeing it. He said he'd be mighty sure to see it, because he'd be a free man the minute he seen it, but if he missed it he'd be in a slave country again and no more show for freedom." –Pp. 91–92

Jim believes he will be free only if they land in Cairo, but in fact, he will still be oppressed by whites. Jim bases his self–worth on the dollar, and it seems that "freedom" is not a state of mind, but rather a state of the Union.

Verbal

Chapter 12

> "'See? He'll be drownded, and won't have nobody to blame for it but his own self. I reckon that's a considerable sight better'n killin' of him. I'm unfavorable to killin' a man as long as you can git aroun' it; it ain't good sense, it ain't good morals. Ain't I right?'"

This misguided man judges it a lesser crime to let a man drown than to kill him outright. Here, Twain satirizes the idiocy and cruelty of human society.

Chapter 20

> "They asked us considerable many questions; wanted to know what we covered up the raft that way for, and laid by in the daytime instead of running—was Jim a runaway nigger? Says I:
>
> 'Goodness sakes, would a runaway nigger run south?'
>
> No, they allowed he wouldn't." –Pg. 127

Huck uses his own mistake to cover up their scheme. He wasn't intentionally going south; but had made a wrong turn.

Chapter 21

> "This is the speech—I learned it, easy enough, while he was learning it to the king:

To be or not to be; that is the bare bodkin

That makes calamity of so long life;

For who would fardels bear..."

Huck, while being impressed to no end with the actors, has gotten the soliloquy entirely wrong, yet another demonstration of his inability to become a member of "civilized" society.

"Then at the bottom was the biggest line of all, which said:
LADIES AND CHILDREN NOT ADMITTED 'There,' says he, 'if that line don't fetch them, I don't know Arkansaw!' –Pg. 150

The duke recognizes and profits from the locals' ignorance and attraction to crass humor.

Chapter 23

"'But Huck, dese kings o' ourn is reglar rapscallions; dat's jist what dey is; dey's reglar rapscallions.'

'Well, that's what I'm a–saying; all kings is mostly rapscallions as fur as I can make out.'

'Is dat so?'

'You read about them once—you'll see. Look at Henry the Eight; this 'n' 's a Sunday–school Superintendent to him.'" –Pg. 153

Huck is under the impression that all kings, or authority figures, for that matter, are corrupt and cruel because of a few examples that have supported this theory. Therefore, their "king's" actions seem minor in comparison to the massive corruption Huck expects.

Chapter 26

"'How is servants treated in England? Do they treat 'em better 'n we treat our niggers?'

'No! A servant ain't nobody there. They treat them worse than dogs.'" –Pg. 172

At this point in America history, slaves were often treated worse than dogs. Throughout the novel, Huck is the only person to acknowledge this unfairness.

Chapter 29

> "'Set down, my boy; I wouldn't strain myself if I was you. I reckon
> you ain't used to lying, it don't seem to come handy; what you want
> is practice. You do it pretty awkward.'" –Pg. 196

Throughout the novel, Huck has survived through lies and dishonesty. Here, he is in
the middle of telling one lie when caught in another.

Chapter 30

> "'But answer me only jest this one more—now don't get mad;
> didn't you have it in your mind to hook the money and hide it?'
>
> The duke never said nothing for a little bit; then he says:
>
> 'Well, I don't care if I did, I didn't do it, anyway. But you not only
> had it in mind to do it, but you done it.'" –Pg. 203

The duke seems guilty about even wanting to commit the crime, while the king, who
committed the act, is accusatory.

Author of ClassicNote and Sources

J. N. Smith, author of ClassicNote. Completed on June 01, 2000, copyright held by GradeSaver.

Updated and revised C. Shelby April 09, 2006. Copyright held by GradeSaver.

Twain, Mark. The Adventures of Huckleberry Finn. New York: Harper and Brothers, 1986.

Twain, Mark. The Adventures of Tom Sawyer. New York: Penguin Classics, 1986.

Essay: Twain's Pre-Civil War America

by Anonymous
September 29, 2001

American authors tend to write about life in their times. Mark Twain lived in the 1800's and witnessed the Civil War era. At that time, our nation was divided over the issue of slavery. The inhumane treatment of slaves moved Twain to use his talent to criticize their treatment. In one of his most famous novels named The Adventures of Huckleberry Finn, Twain depicts the injustice of slavery in the South just before the Civil War.

To begin with, Mark Twain uses the plot of The Adventures of Huckleberry Finn to reveal the truths about life in the South during the 1800's. For starters, slavery proved to be one of the most predominant aspects of southern life at that time. The birth of Mark Twain occurred during this era of slavery, so racism surrounded Twain his whole life.

Twain based his writings upon his own personal experiences. Critics agree that, "The book is a strong voice against racism, but at the same time some passages mirror the values of the racist society Mark was raised in" (Meltzer 89). Secondly, The Adventures of Huckleberry Finn portrays the appalling truths regarding enslavement which pervaded the South. Twain utilizes his work as a means to reveal the factuality of racism. "Perfectly 'nice' people didn't consider the death of a black person worth their notice," claims literary analysts (Salwen). Additionally, Mark Twain illustrates life in the South through the actions of the main character Huckleberry Finn. Huck, as he is known for short, has never perceived slavery as anything but a natural part of life. "Because of his upbringing, the boy starts out believing that slavery is part of the natural order," Salwen exclaims to clarify Huck's ignorance (1). In addition, most of the remaining Southerners possessed the same views of slavery as Huck. "The satire of a decadent slaveholding society gains immensely in force when Mark Twain demonstrates that even the outcast Huck has been in part perverted by it," Smith comments on the oblivious views of Southerners (6:480). Finally, Twain's realistic masterpiece satirizes slavery along with man's quest for freedom.

Since many African–Americans had been imprisoTwainned as slaves, it seems only natural that one would occasionally escape to search for freedom. An obvious quest for freedom in The Adventures of Huckleberry Finn would be that of Jim, an escaped slave. Huck meets Jim and they grow to become exceptional friends. Salwen explains, "It's about a slave who breaks the law and risks his life to win his freedom and be reunited with his family"(1). Huck contributes much aid to Jim's mission for freedom, and thus learns many truths about society. Meltzer elaborates, "Huck helps Jim to escape from slavery, and in a famous scene Huck's spontaneous self is placed in opposition to his acquired conscience,to the prejudices and values of the society he was raised in" (89).

In addition to Jim's pursuit of freedom, Huck hopes for his own independence. By escaping and traveling along the Mississippi River, Huck aspires to gain Freedom for both of them. Unger illustrates, "The next twenty chapters detail adventures on the river or beside the river, in a pattern of withdrawal and return, as Huck and Jim float with their raft toward what they hope will be freedom for both" (203). Huck wishes to prove his independence through his notorious trip along the Mississippi River. "Huckleberry Finn speaks out against stupid conformity and for the freedom and independence of the individual," states Meltzer (89). Naturally, with issues such as slavery and racism pervading his novels, Twain would receive a variety of responses to his works. The Adventures of Huckleberry Finn, like most other novels, has its share of various public responses. First of all, many people respond to the novel in a negative way. For example, some readers possess a feeling of anger towards issues discussed in the novel. One critic elaborates, "The novel's semiliterate narrator, vernacular dialogue,forthright depiction of the hypocrisy and brutality of American life, and unrefined frontier humor were sufficiently radical at the time of its publication to warrant the novel's banishment from numerous libraries as 'the veriest trash'" (19:349). Contrarily, some people do not possess enough knowledge of the issues to understand the novel's message. "It is a concretely liberating effect, and therefore different in kind from Whitman's vision of democracy, which can hardly be said to have been understood by or to have found a response among any considerable number of Americans," explains DeVoto (6:466). On the other hand, many readers have felt positively towards the novel. They believe that The Adventures of Huckleberry Finn has caused society to recognize the mistakes of the past. Hall emphasizes, "Initially a clowning humorist, Twain matured into the role of the seemingly naive wise Fool whose caustic sense of humor forced his audience to recognize humanity's foolishness and society's myriad injustices" (6:452). Along with this recognition came the realization that the treatment of slaves was inhumane. "To its everlasting credit, American society in the postwar period gradually came to the conclusion...that the ancient pattern of discrimination against Negroes was morally and legally indefensible," states Lynn (6:484). Finally, not only does Twain possess a negative view of slavery, he also has a distaste for war.

In conclusion, Mark Twain utilizes the plot in The Adventures of Huckleberry Finn to express the immorality of life in the South during the 1800's. He depicts the code of slavery in the South and the quest for independence of a slave and a young boy. Additionally, Twain's work produced a wide range of readers' responses. Finally,Twain's last major work Pudd'nhead Wilson also strongly spoke out against slavery.

Works Cited

DeVoto, Bernard. "Introduction," The Portable Mark Twain, 1946. Rpt. in Twentieth–Century Literary Criticism, Vol. 6. Detroit:Gale Research Co. 1984, 466.

Lynn, Kenneth. "Welcome Back from the Raft, Huck Honey!" The American Scholar,1977. Rpt. in Twentieth–Century Literary Criticism, Vol. 6, Detroit: Gale

Research Co. 1984, 484.

"Mark Twain," Twentieth–Century Literary Criticism. Vol. 6, 1984 ed. 452.

"Mark Twain," Twentieth–Century Literary Criticism. Vol. 19, 1986 ed. 349.

Meltzer, Milton. Mark Twain: A Writer's Life. New York: Franklin Watts, 1985

Salwen, Peter. Is Huck Finn a Racist Book? New York, NY: Salwen Business
Communication, 1996. Online. Netscape. Available:
http://www.salwen.com/mtrace.html. January 7, 1999.

Smith, Henry. "Mark Twain: The Development of a Writer," The Belknap Press of
Harvard University Press, 1962. Rpt. in Twentieth–Century Literary Criticism, Vol.
6. Detroit: Gale Research Co. 1984, 478.

Unger, Leonard. American Writers IV. New York: Charles Scribner's Sons, 1974.

Essay: Censorship and Classics

by Anonymous
September 05, 2001

Mark Twain, John Steinbeck, Harper Lee, Maya Angelou. What do these writers have in common? Sure, they are all great American authors, but there is something else. They are all "banned." Censored. Forbidden. Who has not read a book by at least one of these authors? All are great pieces of literature and should be crucial parts of the high school curriculum. School censorship of books is detrimental to the educational development of high school students.

In order to understand the problems with school censorship, one must know why it is done. One reason is bad language. A prime example of this type of censorship occurred in a California school when words like ëdamn' and ëhell' were blacked out of Ray Bradbury's Fahrenheit 451. Students were stunned by the irony of the situation. A book about censorship was being censored (Wright). Sexual activity is another common reason for censorship, along with assaults on family values and violence. Why is this happening when 90% of students surveyed do not believe that books should be censored because they contain offensive language or sexual situations (Survey)? Negative racial treatment of characters, setting, or theme also fuels censorship (Simmons).

Something else that must be mentioned in order to understand the evils of school censorship are facts censors ignore; the first being literary quality. When they chose to censor a book they do not take into account the educational value of the book. How can one say a book does not belong in schools if they do not know what lessons it teaches? The second key element ignored is the manner in which teachers lead students to interact with texts. They give no credit to the teachers that they could address an offensive issue, such as slavery, as purely objective. When a teacher teaches controversial issues they usually try to stick to the facts or in a subject like slavery show the evils of it. Teachers are not in schools to fill the minds of children with their own opinions or those of authors. They are there to teach students facts, and the books are instruments in which they do so. The final element ignored by censors is the context of the offensive elements. An example of this is foul language. When a censor looks at a book and sees foul language, they shy away. They do not even consider that this language was the norm during the period in which the story takes place and is thus essential (Simmons).

In today's society the most popular reasons for censorship are racial ones, even though 100% of students surveyed do not believe books should be censored because they contain racial situations (Survey). The prime argument against books containing racially tense situations is that racial slurs "are detrimental to the self esteem of students in minority groups" (Wright). This argument is ridiculous for two reasons. The first is that the slurs add to the realism of the book. "If a book was set in a period of time when racism against blacks was common, then slurs are used by the author to make the reader feel like he/she is actually experiencing the book, rather than reading it" (Wright). The Adventurers of Huckleberry Finn is an example of this. "Doan' le's talk about it, Huck. Po' niggers can't have no luck. I alwuz 'spected dat rattlesnake skin warn't done wit its work" (Twain 97). The derogatory terms in the book are not used to put down African Americans, but to provide valuable insight to the lives and opinions of the people of the pre– emancipated south. The second reason why this argument is ridiculous is because authors sometimes use these slurs to poke fun at the context in which they were used. Thus, at times the slurs are actually used because the author feels racism is bad and is trying to show why.

There are three main reasons that schools should not censor. The first is that a significant benefit of literature is that it provides insights into human experience. The best way to learn about an experience, next to living it, is by reading about it. By censoring books we rob our students of this wellspring of knowledge. The next reason is that as students mature, they benefit by thinking critically about texts. Again, removing these texts is robbing our students. How will students learn about racism without reading Harper Lee's To Kill a Mockingbird? How will they learn the evils of slavery without The Adventurers of Huckleberry Finn? Without these texts, how will they develop their critical thinking skills? We will produce a generation who does not know how to think. The final reason is that censors have no faith in the ability of teachers and students to work through a text critically. Rather, they see nonconforming ideas as dangerous to young and impressionable minds (Simmons). What will we do? If our high school sophomores read Ayn Rand's Anthem they will all denounce democracy, slaughter the American dream, and form a brain dead socialistic society full of cattle with numbers for names and lacking any sort of individuality. For years teachers have used texts with nonconformist themes without creating a generation of foulmouthed communists. Why would they start now? Teachers and students alike know how to take a book, read it, analyze it, and then defend or refute the ideas it contains. When questioned, 100% of students said that when reading a novel containing offensive language, racism, sexual situations etc. that they do not necessarily adopt the words or opinions as their own. 100% also said that students have the ability to read a text, analyze it, and then make an informed decision on whether to agree or disagree with it (Survey). If our students know they can do this, then why do censors not think so?

The main argument of proponents of the censorship of books is ludicrous. They say "letting high schoolers read the material in question will dirty their minds at a time when they are trying to develop their own morals" (Wright). However, the action of not letting highschoolers read such material is itself detrimental to their moral development. To be against something it is first necessary to have a knowledge of it. Censoring and banning books like The Adventurers of Huckleberry Finn denies students this knowledge and this stands against this necessary development.

If censorship is not the answer, than what is? An example would be when the stage adaption of Harper Lee's novel To Kill a Mockingbird was banned at Owings Mills

High School (The Sun). It was banned for two reasons. First "like many works of literature To Kill a Mockingbird makes a moral point by depicting a moral vacuum, the topics it addresses– including rape and racism–create discomfort" (Wright). The other reason is the offensive language used. Simply censoring the book would not work because isolating these words demeans it's intent to condemn racism by illustrating it's worst qualities. Instead, it could have been used as a catalyst for learning, rather than an excuse for continual ignorance. A school wide discussion on race could have taken place after viewing the play and reading the novel. There are alternatives to censorship that have better educational value.

Thus, school censorship of books is detrimental to the educational development of high school students. Mark Twain, John Steinbeck, Harper Lee, Maya Angelou have been teaching our children about controversial issues for generations and look at the effects. We have won two World Wars, squashed communism, pushed through the equal rights movement, ended the Cold War, destroyed the Berlin wall, and stopped Saddam Hussain in his tracks. All done by men and women who read the same books that censors claim promote racism and communism. Even the library says "we support the American Library Association on freedom to read"(Interview). They also say "If parents want materials censored it is up to them, not the government, to do it" (Interview). Students are able to form their own opinion on books and, with the help of teachers, are not going to simply adopt the ideas and vocabulary as their own. "A student has to be taught the various ways of looking at an issue before he or she can decide what side to take" (Wright). That is what novels do. It is the most controversial ones that causes students to think the most. In theory censorship thus prevents students from thinking. There are ways of teaching our children morals, but censorship is not one of them. In the words of Ralph Waldo Emerson, "Every burned book enlightens the world."

Works Cited

Killing a Classic; Censorship: Offensive language can be instructional in a play about racism and segregation. The Sun; Baltimore, Md.; Nov.6, 1999.

Simmons, John S. School Censorship: No Respite in Sight. Forum. Winter 1996/1997, pp. 12–16

Survey. "Survey on Censorship of Books in School" November 18,1999.

Twain, Mark. The Adventurers of Huckleberry Finn. Penguin Books. New York, New York, 1959.

Virginia Beach Public Library Librarian. Interview. November 19, 1999

Wright, Jake. Literary Censorship in America's Schools. On–line. Available: http://members.xoom.com/jakewright/censorship/

Quiz 1

1. **The Adventures of Huckleberry Finn was first published in:**
   A. 1700
   B. 1774
   C. 1800
   D. 1884

2. **The Adventures of Huckleberry Finn can best be described as:**
   A. a social commentary
   B. an epic
   C. an abolitionist novel
   D. a humor novel

3. **Huck Finn and Tom Sawyer each received _____ dollars when they found money that the robbers had hidden in the cave:**
   A. no money
   B. 3,000 dollars
   C. 6,000 dollars
   D. 12,000 dollars

4. **Huck's Pap returns because he:**
   A. misses his son
   B. wants Huck's money
   C. wants revenge on Judge Thatcher
   D. all of the above

5. **When Jim first sees Huck Finn on the island, he thinks Huck:**
   A. has come to arrest him
   B. has run away from home
   C. is a ghost
   D. is trying to bewitch him

6. **Jim runs away from Miss Watson because:**
   A. she is planning to sell him to a slave trader who will take him to New Orleans
   B. he wants to spend time with Huck
   C. he wants to be re-united with his family
   D. he is tired of being a slave

7. **During their travels down the river, Huck talks to Jim about all of the following except:**
    A. royalty
    B. King Solomon
    C. women
    D. money

8. **Tom Sawyer has the other boys form a band of:**
    A. beggars
    B. robbers
    C. pirates
    D. seducers

9. **Huck escapes to Jackson Island and discovers that:**
    A. Miss Watson is there
    B. it is deserted
    C. Pa is there
    D. Jim is there

10. **Mark Twain's approach to the issue of racism in Huckleberry Finn is that:**
    A. he supports it.
    B. he attacks it directly.
    C. he sarcastically denounces it.
    D. he does not deal with the issue of racism in Huckleberry Finn.

11. **The river best serves as a symbol of which of the following?**
    A. freedom
    B. slavery
    C. commerce
    D. equality

12. **The river provides all of the following except:**
    A. money and goods
    B. a permanent home
    C. transportation
    D. food

13. **Jim is all of the following except:**
  A. foolish
  B. superstitious
  C. motherly
  D. hard−working

14. **The narrator of the story is:**
  A. Pa
  B. Jim
  C. Tom
  D. Huck

15. **Huck assumes all of the following identities except:**
  A. George Peters
  B. Sarah Williams
  C. Tom Sawyer
  D. Thomas Smith

16. **Three main symbols are the:**
  A. river, witchcraft, raft
  B. river, money, raft
  C. river, ferryboats, bread
  D. river, names, money

17. **Jim is which of the following during the course of the novel?**
  A. a runaway slave
  B. a free man
  C. Huck's friend
  D. all of the above

18. **Greed is present in all of the following except:**
  A. Jim's financial investments.
  B. The selling of Jim back into slavery.
  C. Pa's return.
  D. The floating bread with quicksilver inside it.

19. **Huck pretends to be _____ when he is caught pretending to be a girl:**
    A. an actor
    B. a boy running away from his abusive father
    C. an escaped apprentice
    D. an escaped convict

20. **The Dauphin represents what historical character?**
    A. a famous actor
    B. the son of the King of England
    C. the son of the Duke
    D. the son of the King of France

21. **The central conflict of the novel is:**
    A. Huck Finn's internal struggle to come to terms with himself and society
    B. getting rid of the Duke and the Dauphin
    C. escaping Pa
    D. freeing Jim from slavery

22. **The Duke and the Dauphin are primarily:**
    A. actors
    B. beggars
    C. thieves
    D. charletans

23. **With whom does Huck start to fall in love in the novel?**
    A. Mary Jane Wilks
    B. Sarah Williams
    C. Huck does not fall in love
    D. Miss Watson

24. **From which family do the Duke and the Dauphin try to steal the inheritance?**
    A. The Wilks
    B. The Phelps
    C. The Grangerfords
    D. The Shepherdsons

25. **Which paradox is inherent in Huck Finn's character?**
    A. he hates money but wants to be rich.
    B. he loves school but hates to learn.
    C. he fully supports slavery but wants to free Jim.
    D. he has a realistic approach to life but is superstitious.

Quiz 1 Answer Key

1. **(D)** 1884
2. **(A)** a social commentary
3. **(C)** 6,000 dollars
4. **(B)** wants Huck's money
5. **(C)** is a ghost
6. **(A)** she is planning to sell him to a slave trader who will take him to New Orleans
7. **(C)** women
8. **(B)** robbers
9. **(D)** Jim is there
10. **(C)** he sarcastically denounces it.
11. **(A)** freedom
12. **(B)** a permanent home
13. **(A)** foolish
14. **(D)** Huck
15. **(D)** Thomas Smith
16. **(B)** river, money, raft
17. **(D)** all of the above
18. **(D)** The floating bread with quicksilver inside it.
19. **(C)** an escaped apprentice
20. **(D)** the son of the King of France
21. **(A)** Huck Finn's internal struggle to come to terms with himself and society
22. **(D)** charletans
23. **(A)** Mary Jane Wilks
24. **(A)** The Wilks
25. **(D)** he has a realistic approach to life but is superstitious.

Quiz 2

1. **Huck kills what animal to convince the town that he has been murdered?**
    A. a chicken
    B. a pig
    C. a cow
    D. a bear

2. **All of the following are used to find dead bodies in the river except:**
    A. divers
    B. dragging the river with nets
    C. firing a cannon over the surface of the water
    D. bread filled with mercury

3. **The dead man that Huck and Jim find on the floating house is:**
    A. the owner of the house
    B. a random dead man
    C. Huck' father
    D. Jim's friend

4. **Jim and Huck are trying to reach which town during their trip downriver?**
    A. Hannibal
    B. no place in particular
    C. Cairo
    D. Grangerford

5. **Huck pretends to be all of the following except:**
    A. a butcher's son
    B. an escaped apprentice
    C. an orphan
    D. a farmer's son

6. **Which Shakespearian plays do the Duke and the Dauphin perform scenes from?**
    A. Romeo and Juliet and Richard III
    B. Hamlet and Macbeth
    C. Romeo and Juliet and Hamlet
    D. Richard II and Hamlet

7. **Twain puts in a scene where Jim tells Huck about his daughter Elizabeth in order to:**

    A. show that Jim misses his family and has identical feelings to white people.

    B. show that Jim is a good father.

    C. show that Jim does not know what it is like to be deaf.

    D. show that Jim is a cruel father who beats up his deaf daughter.

8. **Huck's remark when the Duke and Dauphin pretend to be the brothers of Peter Wilks is, "It was enough to make a body ashamed of the human race." This quote is an example of:**

    A. Huck's growing maturity and disgust with the Duke and Dauphin

    B. Huck's sense of humor

    C. Huck's unwillingness to participate in society.

    D. Huck's shame at being white

9. **The Royal Nonesuch is exactly what the name implies. The fact that it sells out is an example of:**

    A. simile

    B. hyperbole

    C. symbolism

    D. irony

10. **Huck's sense of growing maturity is best described by which of the following quotes:**

    A. "At last she come and begun to ask me questions, but I couldn't answer them straight..." (explaining why he lied to Aunt Sally)

    B. "It was a real bully circus." (describing a circus he attends)

    C. "All right, then, I'll go to hell!" (discussing releasing Jim from slavery)

    D. "I could a stayed if I wanted to, but I didn't want to." (with the Widow)

11. **When Huck meets Aunt Sally for the first time, he makes up what excuse for his being late?**

    A. That the boat he was on went "aground"

    B. That the boat he was on blew out a cylinder–head

    C. That a black man was killed

    D. All of the above

12. **In response to Huck's comment that a black man was killed when the cylinder–head blew, Aunt Sally replies:**

    A. "How terrible! Was anyone else injured?"

    B. "Well, it's terrible; but sometimes people do get hurt."

    C. "Well, it's lucky; because sometimes people do get hurt."

    D. "How awful! Thank goodness no one else was killed."

13. **The final climax of Huck's adventures occurs:**
    A. During the feud when Buck gets killed
    B. At the end when Jim learns that he is free, and Huck learns that his Pa is dead
    C. When Huck and Jim accidentally pass Cairo on the raft
    D. When the raft is run over by a steamboat

14. **There are several revelations at the end of the novel. Which of the following is revealed by Tom Sawyer?**
    A. That Tom was not breaking any laws while freeing Jim
    B. That Jim and Huck are best friends
    C. That Huck's Pa is dead
    D. That Jim is a free man

15. **The fact that Jim knew Huck's Pa was dead but did not tell Huck tells us what about Jim's character?**
    A. That he is might be selfish and wanted to make sure Huck would still run away with him
    B. That Jim's character is complex
    C. That he felt sorry for Huck and wanted to protect him
    D. All of the above

16. **Twain sarcastically portrays religion in all of the following ways except:**
    A. having Huck pray every day while living with the widow
    B. having the Grangerford's carry their guns with them to church
    C. having Huck's prayers get answered
    D. having the King pretend to be a pirate and take advantage of a religious congregation's simplicity

17. **Twain's Huckleberry Finn has been banned for which of the following reasons?**
    A. the close relationship between Huck Finn and Jim
    B. the fear that the book will dirty children's minds
    C. the derogatory use of the word nigger
    D. all of the above

18. **Which character does Huck Finn live with in the opening chapters?**
    A. Widow Douglas
    B. Huck Finn
    C. Jim
    D. Aunt Polly

19. **The Grangerfords are feuding with what family?**
    A. the Wilks
    B. the Shepherdsons
    C. the Watsons
    D. the Jacksons

20. **The feud was started by:**
    A. a Wilks
    B. a Grangerford
    C. a Shepherdson
    D. no one remembers

21. **The feud is best represented by which of the following Shakespeare plays?**
    A. Hamlet
    B. King Lear
    C. Romeo and Juliet
    D. none of the above

22. **What happens to Buck?**
    A. he is killed during the feud
    B. he decides to become a lawyer
    C. he makes Huck leave the Grangerfords
    D. he runs away with one of the Shepherdson girls

23. **Colonel Sherburn is:**
    A. the man who kills Boggs and single–handedly stops an angry mob
    B. the man who tries to protect Boggs and runs to get Boggs' daughter
    C. the man who kills Boggs and has his house ripped down by an angry mob
    D. the man who arrests the Duke and Dauphin

24. **The Duke and the Dauphin are punished by _____:**
    A. life in prison
    B. Huck and Jim
    C. tar and feathering
    D. a fair trial by their peers

25. **Huck and Jim pass Cairo because:**
    A. Huck decides to visit Tom's Aunt Sally
    B. they plan to head further south
    C. there is a thick fog out and they are swept downriver
    D. they are running away from the Duke and Dauphin

Quiz 2 Answer Key

1. (**B**) a pig
2. (**A**) divers
3. (**C**) Huck' father
4. (**C**) Cairo
5. (**A**) a butcher's son
6. (**A**) Romeo and Juliet and Richard III
7. (**A**) show that Jim misses his family and has identical feelings to white people.
8. (**A**) Huck's growing maturity and disgust with the Duke and Dauphin
9. (**D**) irony
10. (**C**) "All right, then, I'll go to hell!" (discussing releasing Jim from slavery)
11. (**D**) All of the above
12. (**C**) "Well, it's lucky; because sometimes people do get hurt."
13. (**B**) At the end when Jim learns that he is free, and Huck learns that his Pa is dead
14. (**D**) That Jim is a free man
15. (**D**) All of the above
16. (**C**) having Huck's prayers get answered
17. (**D**) all of the above
18. (**A**) Widow Douglas
19. (**B**) the Shepherdsons
20. (**D**) no one remembers
21. (**C**) Romeo and Juliet
22. (**A**) he is killed during the feud
23. (**A**) the man who kills Boggs and single–handedly stops an angry mob
24. (**C**) tar and feathering
25. (**C**) there is a thick fog out and they are swept downriver

Quiz 3

1. **In Jim's final escape, who is shot?**
    A. Jim
    B. Tom
    C. Huck
    D. no one

2. **What does Tom make Jim do before escaping?**
    A. live with vermin
    B. write on pieces of metal
    C. scrawl on the walls
    D. all of the above

3. **Who informs everyone that Jim is a free man?**
    A. Tom
    B. Aunt Sally
    C. Huck
    D. Silas

4. **How does Huck know that Pap returned to St. Petersburg?**
    A. He sees his footprints in the snow
    B. He hears rumors in town
    C. He sees his boat tied near the dock
    D. Tom tells him

5. **What is Jim's destination when he starts downriver?**
    A. The Ohio River
    B. St. Louis
    C. unknown
    D. New Orleans

6. **Which Grangerford sister elopes?**
    A. Sophia
    B. Mary Jane
    C. Susan
    D. Joanna

7. What is inside the witch pie that Tom and Huck bake for Jim?

    A. Snakes

    B. A rope of knotted sheet

    C. Meat

    D. Fruit

8. What charm does Jim wear around his neck?

    A. five–cent piece

    B. hairball

    C. pig's tooth

    D. rabbit's foot

9. What is Mark Twain's real name?

    A. Samuel Clemes

    B. George Howell

    C. Robert Sandborn

    D. Samuel Finn

10. At the end of the novel, what are Huck's intentions?

    A. stay with Aunt Sally

    B. continue downriver

    C. head West

    D. move in with Tom and Aunt Polly

11. Huck stays with the following family on his journey

    A. Wilks's

    B. Grangerford's

    C. Phelps's

    D. All of the above

12. Rather than turn Jim in, Huck claims

    A. he has been kidnapped

    B. in fact, he turns Jim in

    C. his family needs help and has smallpox

    D. he is lost and alone

13. What act of bad luck does Huck commit?

A. touches a dead snake skin

B. burns a spider to death in a candle flame

C. spills salt

D. All of the above

14. What do Jim and Huck use to travel downriver?

A. canoe and a raft

B. steamboat only

C. raft only

D. canoe only

15. Jim's primary concern is

A. freedom

B. saving his family

C. being alive

D. money

16. When pretending to be a girl, Huck reveals himself by

A. demonstrating perfect aim

B. failing to thread a needle properly

C. bringing his knees together to catch something in his lap

D. All of the above

17. Huck finds what source of food when the town is searching for his dead body?

A. A butchered pig

B. Baked potatoes

C. Fresh vegetables

D. A fresh loaf of bread

18. What does Huck use to escape the cabin?

A. hammer

B. wrench

C. hatchet

D. saw

19. **Huck's first reaction upon discovering someone else is on Jackson's Island is to**
    A. search the person out

    B. run home

    C. flee

    D. stand guard to wait for the person to return to the campfire

20. **In debating heaven and hell, Huck decides**
    A. he doesn't believe in either

    B. he would rather go to heaven

    C. he would rather go to hell

    D. he is unsure

21. **What girl does Huck develop somewhat of a crush on?**
    A. Mary Jane Wilks

    B. Aunt Sally

    C. Aunt Polly

    D. Sophia Grangerford

22. **What is the Royal Nonesuch?**
    A. Huck's name for his and Jim's journey

    B. a Shakespearian drama

    C. a scam production put on my the Duke and King

    D. The name of the raft

23. **Where does Huck hide the Wilks money?**
    A. in his clothes

    B. in the coffin

    C. underground

    D. under his bed

24. **What tattoo was on Peter Wilks's chest?**
    A. none

    B. a blue arrow

    C. a tree

    D. his initials

25. **After their journey through the fog**

    A. Huck and Jim are forced to walk along the banks as their raft and canoe were destroyed

    B. Huck pretends it was all a dream

    C. Jim is lost forever

    D. Huck almost drowns

Quiz 3 Answer Key

1. **(B)** Tom
2. **(D)** all of the above
3. **(A)** Tom
4. **(A)** He sees his footprints in the snow
5. **(A)** The Ohio River
6. **(A)** Sophia
7. **(B)** A rope of knotted sheet
8. **(A)** five–cent piece
9. **(A)** Samuel Clemes
10. **(C)** head West
11. **(D)** All of the above
12. **(C)** his family needs help and has smallpox
13. **(D)** All of the above
14. **(A)** canoe and a raft
15. **(A)** freedom
16. **(D)** All of the above
17. **(D)** A fresh loaf of bread
18. **(D)** saw
19. **(C)** flee
20. **(C)** he would rather go to hell
21. **(A)** Mary Jane Wilks
22. **(C)** a scam production put on my the Duke and King
23. **(B)** in the coffin
24. **(D)** his initials
25. **(B)** Huck pretends it was all a dream

Quiz 4

1. **When does Jim become free?**
   A. when he runs away from Miss Watson
   B. when Miss Watson dies
   C. never
   D. when he escapes from the hut at the Phelps's farm

2. **What do Tom and Huck steal from Aunt Sally?**
   A. a sheet
   B. a spoon
   C. candles
   D. all of the above

3. **What do Tom and Jim collect for Jim's hut?**
   A. snakes
   B. bugs
   C. rats
   D. all of the above

4. **What does the slave tell Huck he wants to show him when bringing him to Jim?**
   A. a hideout
   B. Jim
   C. water moccasins
   D. rats

5. **Huck is almost not allowed to join Tom's band of robbers because**
   A. he does not have a family
   B. he can't pay
   C. he makes fun of Tom
   D. he isn't interested

6. **On the day before the feud, what is the church sermon about?**
   A. honoring thy father
   B. honesty
   C. brotherly love
   D. the perils of hell

7. **What is hidden in Sophia Grangerford's testament?**
    A. nothing
    B. money
    C. a lock of hair
    D. a note from her Shepherdson lover

8. **Who does Huck see dead?**
    A. Jim
    B. Aunt Sally
    C. Buck
    D. Miss Watson

9. **When does Huck cry?**
    A. pulling Buck's body from the river
    B. running from Pap for the last time
    C. when he reunites with Tom again
    D. when he thinks he has lost Jim in the fog

10. **What does Huck steal?**
    A. whiskey
    B. food
    C. a boat
    D. All of the above

11. **What happened to Jim's daughter?**
    A. she lost her hearing
    B. she died
    C. she married young
    D. she ran away

12. **Who reveals Huck and Tom's identities at the Phelps home?**
    A. Jim
    B. Tom
    C. Aunt Polly
    D. Huck

13. **Is Huck afraid of the river?**
    A. Yes, the currents are strong and dangerous
    B. Yes, he can't swim
    C. No
    D. Yes, he knows Jim will be caught

14. **What do Huck and Jim build on the raft to improve it?**
    A. ladder down the side
    B. large roof
    C. teepee hut
    D. four extra levels of wood

15. **How far does the raft make it?**
    A. all the way downriver
    B. only as far as Jackson's Island
    C. until the steamboat crashes into it
    D. the Duke and Dauphin steal it after the final Royal Nonesuch
    production

16. **Who tells Silas about the Royal Nonesuch?**
    A. Jim
    B. Tom
    C. Aunt Sally
    D. Huck

17. **This novel has been perceived as**
    A. racist
    B. anti−southern
    C. anti−religious
    D. all of the above

18. **When planning his escape, who knows Jim is free?**
    A. Tom
    B. Aunt Sally
    C. Huck
    D. Silas

19. **What do the Duke and King disguise Jim as?**
    A. they don't disguise him, but keep him hidden
    B. their personal slave
    C. sick arab
    D. shackled runaway slave

20. **Who gives Jim to the Phelps?**
    A. Tom
    B. King
    C. Huck
    D. Duke

21. **Upon arriving at the Phelps home, why is Huck relieved?**
    A. The Phelps help him find Jim and lead him to safety
    B. He considers his journey over and decides to live with the Phelps's and forget about Jim
    C. Aunt Sally is Tom's aunt and believes Huck is Tom
    D. Tom is there, waiting to greet him

22. **Who is anti–slavery in this novel?**
    A. Tom
    B. Aunt Sally
    C. Huck
    D. Miss Watson

23. **Who is a true friend to Huck?**
    A. the Duke
    B. Jim
    C. Tom
    D. Aunt Sally

24. **In Tom and Huck's relationship, who is the leader?**
    A. neither
    B. Tom
    C. Huck
    D. both

25. **In this novel, who dies?**
    A. Pap
    B. Buck
    C. steamboat robbers
    D. all of the above

Quiz 4 Answer Key

1. **(B)** when Miss Watson dies
2. **(D)** all of the above
3. **(D)** all of the above
4. **(C)** water moccasins
5. **(A)** he does not have a family
6. **(C)** brotherly love
7. **(D)** a note from her Shepherdson lover
8. **(C)** Buck
9. **(A)** pulling Buck's body from the river
10. **(D)** All of the above
11. **(A)** she lost her hearing
12. **(C)** Aunt Polly
13. **(C)** No
14. **(C)** teepee hut
15. **(A)** all the way downriver
16. **(A)** Jim
17. **(D)** all of the above
18. **(A)** Tom
19. **(C)** sick arab
20. **(B)** King
21. **(C)** Aunt Sally is Tom's aunt and believes Huck is Tom
22. **(C)** Huck
23. **(B)** Jim
24. **(B)** Tom
25. **(D)** all of the above

ClassicNotes

GrAdeSaver™

Getting you the grade since 1999™

Other ClassicNotes from GradeSaver™

1984
Absalom, Absalom
Adam Bede
The Adventures of Augie
    March
The Adventures of
    Huckleberry Finn
The Adventures of Tom
    Sawyer
The Aeneid
Agamemnon
The Age of Innocence
Alice in Wonderland
All My Sons
All Quiet on the Western
    Front
All the King's Men
All the Pretty Horses
The Ambassadors
American Beauty
Angela's Ashes
Animal Farm
Anna Karenina
Antigone
Antony and Cleopatra
Aristotle's Ethics
Aristotle's Poetics
Aristotle's Politics
As I Lay Dying
As You Like It
The Awakening
Babbitt
The Bacchae
Bartleby the Scrivener
The Bean Trees
The Bell Jar

Beloved
Benito Cereno
Beowulf
Billy Budd
Black Boy
Bluest Eye
Brave New World
Breakfast at Tiffany's
Call of the Wild
Candide
The Canterbury Tales
Cat's Cradle
Catch-22
The Catcher in the Rye
The Caucasian Chalk
    Circle
The Cherry Orchard
The Chosen
A Christmas Carol
Chronicle of a Death
    Foretold
Civil Disobedience
Civilization and Its
    Discontents
A Clockwork Orange
The Color of Water
The Color Purple
Comedy of Errors
Communist Manifesto
A Confederacy of
    Dunces
Connecticut Yankee in
    King Arthur's Court
Coriolanus
The Count of Monte
    Cristo

Crime and Punishment
The Crucible
Cry, the Beloved
    Country
The Crying of Lot 49
Cymbeline
Daisy Miller
Death in Venice
Death of a Salesman
The Death of Ivan Ilych
Democracy in America
Devil in a Blue Dress
The Diary of Anne Frank
Disgrace
Divine Comedy-I:
    Inferno
A Doll's House
Don Quixote Book I
Don Quixote Book II
Dr. Faustus
Dr. Jekyll and Mr. Hyde
Dracula
Dubliners
East of Eden
Emma
Endgame
Ethan Frome
The Eumenides
Everything is Illuminated
Fahrenheit 451
The Fall of the House of
    Usher
Farewell to Arms
The Federalist Papers
For Whom the Bell Tolls
The Fountainhead

For our full list of over 250 Study Guides, Quizzes,
Sample College Application Essays, Literature Essays and E-texts, visit:

www.gradesaver.com

ClassicNotes

GradeSaver™

Getting you the grade since 1999™

Other ClassicNotes from GradeSaver™

Frankenstein
Franny and Zooey
Glass Menagerie
The God of Small Things
The Grapes of Wrath
Great Expectations
The Great Gatsby
Hamlet
The Handmaid's Tale
Hard Times
Heart of Darkness
Hedda Gabler
Henry IV (Pirandello)
Henry IV Part 1
Henry IV Part 2
Henry V
The Hobbit
Homo Faber
House of Mirth
House of the Seven
    Gables
House on Mango Street
Howards End
A Hunger Artist
I Know Why the Caged
    Bird Sings
An Ideal Husband
Iliad
The Importance of Being
    Earnest
In Our Time
Inherit the Wind
Invisible Man
The Island of Dr. Moreau
Jane Eyre
Jazz

The Joy Luck Club
Julius Caesar
Jungle of Cities
Kidnapped
King Lear
Last of the Mohicans
Leviathan
Libation Bearers
The Lion, the Witch and
    the Wardrobe
Lolita
Long Day's Journey Into
    Night
Lord Jim
Lord of the Flies
The Lord of the Rings:
    The Fellowship of the
    Ring
The Lord of the Rings:
    The Return of the
    King
The Lord of the Rings:
    The Two Towers
A Lost Lady
The Love Song of J.
    Alfred Prufrock
Lucy
Macbeth
Madame Bovary
Manhattan Transfer
Mansfield Park
The Mayor of
    Casterbridge
Measure for Measure
Medea
Merchant of Venice

Metamorphoses
The Metamorphosis
Middlemarch
Midsummer Night's
    Dream
Moby Dick
Moll Flanders
Mother Courage and Her
    Children
Mrs. Dalloway
Much Ado About
    Nothing
My Antonia
Native Son
Night
No Exit
Notes from Underground
O Pioneers
The Odyssey
Oedipus Rex / Oedipus
    the King
Of Mice and Men
The Old Man and the Sea
On Liberty
One Day in the Life of
    Ivan Denisovich
One Flew Over the
    Cuckoo's Nest
One Hundred Years of
    Solitude
Oroonoko
Othello
Our Town
Pale Fire
Paradise Lost
A Passage to India

For our full list of over 250 Study Guides, Quizzes,
Sample College Application Essays, Literature Essays and E-texts, visit:

www.gradesaver.com

ClassicNotes

GradeSaver™

Getting you the grade since 1999™

Other ClassicNotes from GradeSaver™

The Pearl
The Picture of Dorian Gray
Poems of W.B. Yeats: The Rose
Portrait of the Artist as a Young Man
Pride and Prejudice
Prometheus Bound
Pudd'nhead Wilson
Pygmalion
Rabbit, Run
A Raisin in the Sun
Red Badge of Courage
The Republic
Richard II
Richard III
The Rime of the Ancient Mariner
Robinson Crusoe
Roll of Thunder, Hear My Cry
Romeo and Juliet
A Room of One's Own
A Room With a View
Rosencrantz and Guildenstern Are Dead
Salome
The Scarlet Letter
Secret Sharer
Sense and Sensibility
A Separate Peace
Shakespeare's Sonnets
Siddhartha
Silas Marner

Sir Gawain and the Green Knight
Sister Carrie
Six Characters in Search of an Author
Slaughterhouse Five
Snow Falling on Cedars
Something Wicked This Way Comes
Song of Roland
Sons and Lovers
The Sorrows of Young Werther
The Sound and the Fury
Spring Awakening
The Stranger
A Streetcar Named Desire
The Sun Also Rises
Tale of Two Cities
The Taming of the Shrew
The Tempest
Tender is the Night
Tess of the D'Urbervilles
Their Eyes Were Watching God
Things Fall Apart
The Threepenny Opera
The Time Machine
Titus Andronicus
To Build a Fire
To Kill a Mockingbird
To the Lighthouse
Treasure Island
Troilus and Cressida
Turn of the Screw

Twelfth Night
Ulysses
Uncle Tom's Cabin
Utopia
A Very Old Man With Enormous Wings
The Visit
Volpone
Waiting for Godot
Waiting for Lefty
Walden
Washington Square
Where the Red Fern Grows
White Fang
White Noise
White Teeth
Who's Afraid of Virginia Woolf
Winesburg, Ohio
The Winter's Tale
Woyzeck
Wuthering Heights
The Yellow Wallpaper
Yonnondio: From the Thirties

For our full list of over 250 Study Guides, Quizzes,
Sample College Application Essays, Literature Essays and E-texts, visit:

www.gradesaver.com

Made in the USA
Columbia, SC
24 November 2018